An Innocent Girl

A MEMOIR BY

CHRISTINE TEMLETT

AN INNOCENT GIRL

Copyright © 2020 by Christine Temlett.

All rights reserved. No part of this book may be used or reproduced in any manner whatsoever without written permission except in the case of brief quotations embodied in critical articles or reviews.

Although this is a work of non-fiction, some people's names have been changed in the book to protect their identities. Place names also have been changed.

You can contact Christine Temlett on Twitter, @Chrisie2811, or Facebook, https://www.facebook.com/christine.temlett

Book and Cover design by Your Memoir

ISBN: 9798570810259
Imprint: Independently published

First Edition: November 2020

An Innocent Girl

Prologue

NOVEMBER 28, 1945

"HURRY, SAM. HURRY! Your mother needs the midwife."

Jack's voice, usually so calm, was desperate, prompting his son to grab his bike and race towards the village. Jack returned to the bedroom to try and comfort his wife. "I've sent Sam up to get the midwife, Ruby," he said, wiping her brow and praying silently for Sam's speedy return as she cried out in pain.

Good lad, he thought, gripping Ruby's hand. Soon he heard the bicycles outside the Fir Tree Cottage.

'Good lad,' he said out loud, as he walked into the kitchen to find Sam and Nurse Green. His other son, Tim, burst into the kitchen to find them all rushing up the stairs. The boys, aged 12 and 14, who worried about their mother, as at 43, she was rather old to be having a baby, made to follow up the stairs.

"You two, out now," Jack shouted down at them.

The sound of her cries made both feel uneasy, but they

turned away and walked out. Sam suggested going for a walk to take his younger brother's mind off the situation. They made their way across the road and climbed over the hedge into the field. A few cows looked up from their grazing and started mooing. The imposing white hills of the nearby china clay works dominated the landscape, in stark contrast to the gorse and heather of the Cornish moorland surrounding Fir Tree Cottage.

The boys gazed back towards the cottage, hoping their mother was delivering a much-wanted daughter, before they started picking hazelnuts from the hedgerow.

"They will be nice to eat at Christmas," said Tim, stuffing his pockets.

"They're a good colour," said Sam. "Yellow and brown, really ripe. I can't believe it's only a month away."

"Yes, and Mum loves these nuts. We can roast them by the fire."

Just then a baby began to wail. The boys looked at each other, stuffed a few final nuts into their pockets and ran for home.

Their father was trotting down the stairs as they barrelled into the porch. "It's good news!" he said. "You have a baby sister."

Nurse Green appeared at the top of the stairs. "Do you want to see her, boys?"

Sam and Tim kicked off their shoes, raced upstairs and rushed into the bedroom, where their mother was cradling the new arrival.

"Isn't she gorgeous!" said Sam. "So tiny and really cute."

"She's like a little doll," said Tim. "What's her name?"

Jack smiled at Ruby. "Your mother has decided she wants to call her Christine."

The boys agreed it was a lovely name. Sam said he was going up to Mill Hill to tell Aunty Alice and Uncle Will. He ran all the way and made it in record time, stopping for just a second to pat Aunty Alice's collie, Lassie, before knocking on the door.

When Alice answered, Sam could barely get his words out quickly enough. "Aunty Alice, Aunty Alice..." he gasped, panting for breath. "Mum's just had a baby girl... I've got a little sister."

Sam beamed at Aunty Alice, proud and delighted at being the one to tell her the good news about her sister. Uncle Will came to the door and invited Sam in. He followed them into the sitting room, neat and tidy as always, where Aunty Alice had been knitting baby clothes and Uncle Will reading the newspaper. Sam sniffed the air. Aunty Alice had been making her marvellous pasties again, but Sam wasn't distracted. "She's called Christine!" he said. "She's so sweet, absolutely perfect."

Aunty Alice and Uncle Will smiled at each other. They were proud of Sam, who had done well at school and had just started an apprenticeship at a garage.

"We know you'll be a great brother," said Uncle Will.

"Stop and have a pasty and a cup of tea," said Aunty Alice. Sam couldn't resist, but after he'd eaten and told his aunt and uncle everything he knew about the baby, and the latest about his job at the garage, he made his excuses.

"I want to go and see Uncle Tom and Aunty Mary," he said. "I want to catch them before opening time."

Mum's brother Tom, and his wife Mary, ran the Jolly Miller

Inn, with Tom also running a taxi business alongside.

Alice and Will followed Sam down the garden path to wave him off.

"Tell your mother I'll be down to see her tomorrow," said Alice. "I can't wait to see my new baby niece and I'll bring the clothes I've knitted. I'll write and tell your cousin Victoria too. She'll be so excited to see the baby when she comes home from teacher training college for Christmas."

Sam made his way up the winding hill to the main road, passing the old abandoned stone quarry before heading into the village. He strode pass the village church and soon the white stone-washed walls of the Jolly Miller were just ahead of him. He knew Tom and Mary would be delighted with the news. The pub was shut, so Sam went round the back where he spotted Uncle Tom and Aunty Mary feeding the pigs they kept in the back yard.

"Uncle Tom, Aunty Mary! Mum's had a baby girl," he shouted.

"Wonderful, Sam. That's the best news I've heard in ages," called Tom over the sound of his snorting pigs. "I know Ruby was hoping for a girl."

"We're all delighted," said Sam. "It'll be a great Christmas. Dad's already sorting out the best turkey."

"This calls for a celebration at the Jolly Miller tonight to wet the baby's head," Aunty Mary announced.

Sam smiled, knowing it wouldn't be long before news of the baby had reached the entire village. "I've got some nappies and bibs I bought last time I was in town," said Mary. "You can take them home with you, Sam."

"That's really lovely," he said as Aunty Mary disappeared into the pub before returning with a bag. She and Uncle Tom didn't have children of their own but were exceedingly kind to their nieces and nephews.

"Before I forget, Sam, could you please ask your father to sort me out a nice-sized goose for Christmas?" she asked. Ruby and Jack reared their own turkeys, geese, ducks and chickens, and Sam assured her his father would provide the ideal bird.

"Right, I better head home to see that little sister of mine," he said.

"Before you leave, how's work at the garage?" asked Tom.

"I'm really enjoying it."

"Good. I'm waiting for the day when you can repair my taxi when it breaks down," said Tom.

"I'd be glad to help," said Sam. "That's what families are for."

It wasn't long before Sam was back home gazing down at his newborn sister as she slept in her cot.

"If anybody lays a finger on you, they'll have me to answer to," he whispered to her. "I'd kill anyone who ever dared to hurt you."

Chapter One

"HURRY UP, CHRISTINE, hurry up and put your boots on."

I kicked off my slippers, put on my new red Wellington boots and followed Mum out of the door.

"That's a good girl," she said, handing me a bag of seed. "You can help feed the chickens."

When we arrived at the chicken pen, the birds came clucking over to greet us. We sprinkled corn and maze on the ground and I watched my mother collect the eggs and place them gently in a basket. "We'll put these eggs in the pantry," she said. "Then we'll go and feed the geese and ducks."

As usual we received a noisy welcome from the geese.

"They sound very hungry, Mummy," I said, making my way to the little stream which ran through the enclosure, where my mother joined me after she'd finished feeding the birds. "Look at the fish!" I said.

"They're minnows, Christine," she told me.

I stood mesmerized by these silver creatures, darting between the stones.

"Turkeys now, they must be starving!"

I followed Mum through the garden gate and into the field where we kept the turkeys. At three years old, I found the cacophony of gobbling sounds erupting from the rafter of turkeys completely overwhelming.

"They make a funny noise, Mummy," I shouted.

"They're just different, Christine. But they are beautiful turkeys, the best for miles around."

I knew my mother was proud of her turkeys, but I felt nervous. Some of them were as big as me, and I stayed close to her until it was time to go. I watched as she secured the gate, then she bent down to me. "I don't know what I would do without you, Christine," she said. "You're a lovely little helper."

I felt so pleased and skipped back towards the cottage. "I like helping you, Mummy," I said.

"Your father will be home from work soon. He's on early shift today," she said.

I was skipping even faster now I loved it when father was home early.

Back indoors, Tim was standing by the table, as always, the pockets of his trousers bulging. I always wondered what he carried in his pockets, it made him look funny. Sometimes he would pull out a watch, seeing that he could now repair them, like a proper jeweller. This time I could see something like the corner of a wooden box sticking out of his pocket. I made a beeline for it and snatched it out of his pocket, laughing and running away with it.

It looked odd and I couldn't make out what it was in the short time I had it, before Tim caught up with me and grabbed my hair, making me stop. I started screaming however his screams were louder than mine.

"Don't touch this ever again!" he shouted, his face inches from mine. I felt his spit pelting my cheeks as he screamed.

Mum rushed over to us and forced his hand to let go of my hair. By then, I was sobbing in pain and scared stiff. I had never seen him like this before.

He finally pushed me hard to the floor and walked out of the house.

"Are you all right, Christine?" Mum asked, trying to comfort me in her arms. I was however having none of it and carried on with my shocked wailing.

"Listen to me, my love," Mum said, looking straight into my eyes. "Listen to me. What you took from Tim is a very precious thing. It's an old pin ball game his best friend, David, gifted him. Remember David? I told you about him."

I shook my head.

"When Tim was about seven or eight, remember?"

I shook my head again.

"David was Tim's best friend and he died as a crumbling wall fell on top of him, right in front of Tim's eyes."

* * *

It wasn't long before I heard the familiar sound of my father's motorbike pulling up. I rushed outside and as soon as Dad had placed his bike securely on its stand, he bent down, picked me up, gave me a hug and carried me back into the cottage.

"I'm glad you're home, Jack," said Mum. "I'll put the kettle on. Would you get some water from the well?"

"Of course," he said.

I followed my father as I wanted to watch him draw water from the well. It was fun seeing him wind the bucket down then turn the handle to bring it up again, the water sloshing from side to side with some of it dropping back down the well.

"Keep back," he said. "It's very deep."

"I won't get too close, Daddy," I promised, watching as he drew two buckets of water.

He carefully closed the wooden lid and placed an enormous stone on top of it. He looked at me. "Don't want to take any chances, now we have you around."

We went into the kitchen and Mum gave him a cup of tea and me a beaker of milk.

"Will you tell me a story, Daddy?" I asked. I enjoyed sitting on my father's lap and listening to stories.

"Not now, love," he said. "I've got some work to do in the garden." He could see the disappointment on my face and delved into his crib bag. "See what your old dad has brought you home today, Christine?" he said, handing me a beautiful purple stone he'd found while hosing down the clay at work. It sparkled in the light and I was entranced.

"Thank you, Daddy," I said, giving him a huge hug. "I'll put it on the windowsill where I can watch it sparkle in the sun."

"You can help me with the baking, Christine," said Mum.

I felt happy to help her bake as I enjoyed rolling out the

pastry. Mum was going to make biscuits and I watched as she got out her mixing bowl, rolling pin and pastry board, and placed them on the big farmhouse table.

"I'm off out to the garden," said Dad, planting a kiss on the top of my head. "I'll be looking forward to having a biscuit after tea, Christine, especially if you make gingerbread men."

Mum began making scones and saffron buns, both favourites with the family. I was allowed to stir the mixture with a wooden spoon. When the mixture was ready and in the oven, she said we were going to make gingerbread men. I loved them as they tasted really hot and spicy. I helped her mix the ingredients in the bowl, then roll it out and use the cutter to shape the biscuits.

I knew my big brothers, Sam and Tim, liked gingerbread men too, and I asked Mum when they would be home, Sam from the garage and Tim from the jewellers in town, where he had started working since leaving school. He was an apprentice, learning how to repair clocks and watches. My parents were proud of them both for getting apprenticeships and my father was happy they wouldn't be following him into the clay works, where the work was tough and the pay poor.

"Not long now love, so I'll clean up and start cooking tea," she said. She scrubbed the table and soon the smell of sausage and mash was making me hungry, but I knew Mum would make me wait until we were all sat together. I was excited when my brothers arrived home. I waited at the table as they washed their hands.

"Smells good, Mum," said Sam.

"Yes, we're starving," said Tim.

I got up and placed the plate of gingerbread men on the table, wanting them to know I had been busy too. They looked pleased and said how much they loved gingerbread men. Dad came in from the garden and Mum asked him to light the oil lamp as it was getting dark, and its glow was soon casting shadows on the walls. Keen to entertain me, my brothers started making shadow puppets on the walls. I giggled in amazement as Tim made the shape of a cat appear and I could see its ears wiggling.

"Look at my rabbit, Christine!" said Sam. I was delighted to see a rabbit hopping along the wall and even more surprised when it did an enormous hop and disappeared behind the curtain.

"Where did the rabbit go?" I asked, but everyone was too busy tucking into their sausage and mash to answer. Not a scrap of food was left when we'd finished eating. I handed the gingerbread men round and we were enjoying them with a cup of tea when, from nowhere, Sam announced, "I've decided to give up my job at the garage and join the RAF."

I heard Mum gasp and Dad splutter. There was a pause until my father said, "I don't think you will like the RAF, Sam. It will be difficult for you to accept the discipline."

Sam looked annoyed. "Don't be so bloody stupid, old man," he snapped. "You're talking rubbish."

The room fell dead silent. I was frightened and started to shake. I'd never heard Sam speak like this before. I was sitting next to Mum and held onto her skirt. She'd stopped eating her biscuit and looked shocked at Sam's sudden outburst.

Sam glared at Dad. "It's different now. Things have changed since you were in the Army."

"You should give it a bit more thought, Sam. You've only got another 12 months to go and you'll be a fully qualified mechanic."

It was as if he had put a match to gunpowder. Sam raised his fist and slammed it down on the table. His plate jumped up, smashing onto the floor. "No need for you to get nasty, Sam," said Dad, his voice still calm but sounding nervous as he remained in his seat at the table. Mum looked disapprovingly at Sam.

"I'm fed up with working in the garage," snapped Sam. "And don't think I'm going to take any notice of an old man like you."

"Right," said Mum, getting to her feet. "Sam, don't talk to your father like that. Can't you see your behaviour is frightening Christine? I really think it would be a good idea to finish your apprenticeship."

Sam knew Mum was really the one in charge of the house, but he continued to protest. "No!" he said. "My mind's made up and there's nothing you or the old man can do about it. The garage has promised to give me a good reference, so I won't have any problems getting in."

With that he kicked back his chair and stormed upstairs to his room. Tim had a grin on his face, almost as if he had enjoyed the row. He got up and followed Sam. I sat shivering as Mum started to clear the plate that Sam had smashed. Dad got up to help her and when they were finished, he asked me if I would like a bedtime story.

"Yes please, Daddy," I said.

"Joseph and his coat of many colours, I think," he said. "It's one your grandfather used to tell me."

I enjoyed the story. "Wasn't it kind of Joseph to be so good to his brothers after the way he was treated?" I asked.

"Yes, I suppose so Christine," said Dad. "Sleep tight."

A few months later Sam arrived home in his RAF uniform having been based at St Eval with the Coastal Command. He looked so smart, complete with slicked-back haircut, that I couldn't help feeling proud of him.

"I'm ground staff based at St Eval" he told us. "My job is to check and maintain the aircraft. I'm working with a really decent bunch of chaps."

Tim looked impressed and Mum seemed much happier. Soon after that Sam bought a motorbike and I could not help noticing it was bigger and better than the one Dad had.

* * *

I was always pleased when Sam arrived home on weekend leave. He would often pick me up, put me on his shoulders, and carry me around the house and the garden.

"Where's Sam?" I asked Mum one day.

"In the garden, dear," she said. "Go and look for him."

It wasn't long before I spotted Sam hiding between the pea vines, eating the peas. "Do you want a few peas, Christine?" he asked.

"Daddy told me we're not allowed to eat them," I said.

"Oh, he won't mind us having a few."

I stood beside Sam shelling and eating peas, and it wasn't until I heard him shout that I realised he had crept away.

"Come down here, Dad," he called. "Christine's pinching the peas."

I was frightened and tried to hide, but it was too late, Dad was already on his way down the path towards me.

"Christine, what are you doing?" He looked and sounded very cross. "You know I told you that you mustn't eat the garden peas."

"I only started eating them because I saw Sam eating them," I said.

Sam was grinning at the other end of the garden and it must have dawned on Dad what he was up to.

"Come on then, Christine. I told you if you keep eating the peas, there won't be any left for our dinner."

Sam sniggered at me as we walked back towards the cottage. "You got caught, didn't you?" he teased. I scowled at him. I felt cross with him and his cheeky grin. I ran indoors to tell Mum.

"Whatever will you pair be up to next?" she said. "Sam's old enough to know better, he's the one who should be told off."

I was glad Mum was on my side. "I love you, Mummy," I said, as she sat down in her armchair and I climbed on her knee.

"Wednesday tomorrow Christine, the day Aunty Alice comes down to visit."

"Great," I shouted excitedly. "I love Aunty Alice."

I spotted Sam out on the back step and noticed he had the shoe polish in one hand and his shoes in the other. I climbed off Mum's knee as I wanted to watch him doing what he called "spit and polish". I watched as he put the polish on the shoes and spit on them, before buffing them to a shine with the shoe brush. He sounded in good spirits and started singing: "On top of old Smokey all covered in snow..." It was good listening to him singing.

"Got to look my best, we've got an inspection in the morning," he said to Mum.

"Well, being in the air force has certainly smartened you up son," she said smiling proudly.

Sam winked at me. "Hey, little sis. I'm flying to Dublin next week and I'll bring you back a lovely Irish doll."

I jumped up and down in excitement, forgiving him instantly for getting me in trouble.

Next day Aunty Alice arrived as promised. She greeted me, as always, by saying, "Christine, my favourite niece," before inviting us to tea that Sunday.

"Victoria and Edward have an announcement," she said, referring to Victoria's boyfriend who she'd met at teacher training college.

"Have they decided to get engaged?" asked Mum.

"You'll have to wait until Sunday. Victoria and Edward would like to tell you themselves! I'll send Tom down in his taxi at 4pm to collect you."

"Are Tom and Mary coming too?" asked Mum.

"Yes, Mary's sister will be taking over at the Jolly Miller."

"Great! Sam's home too," said Mum. "He can come along."

I continued playing as Mum and Aunty Alice chatted about family news and village gossip, until Alice went home leaving Mum and me looking forward to Sunday.

Chapter Two

IT WAS ME who woke the household up on Sunday morning. As usual, Tim and Sam were not pleased. I knew Dad would ask them to get dressed and walk to church.

Tim in particular didn't want to go because a group of boys from the next village would hide in the bushes and throw stones at them when they got near the church.

If they didn't go, Dad would kick their backsides until they relented and went. So they had dad one end kicking them and the boys the other end lying in wait for them.

This Sunday they weren't going to go church, as they needed to get ready for the visit to Aunty Alice's.

At 4pm, Uncle Tom beeped the horn of his taxi and all five of us went out and got in his car. I sat on Mum's lap on the back seat and enjoyed the ride. I admired Aunty Alice's pretty front lawn with pink and white flowers when we arrived at the bungalow. Sam and I made a fuss of Lassie before we went inside and saw an amazing spread of sandwiches, sausage rolls, jellies and lots of other tasty treats. Victoria stood up and came over to greet us.

"I'd like you to meet Edward," she said, introducing him.

"You must be Christine," Edward said to me. "Victoria told me she had a beautiful little cousin." Edward was tall, dark and handsome. I felt in awe and much too shy to speak to him.

"Come here, Christine," said Victoria, holding her arms out to me. I ran over to her. "We have lots of nice things to eat," she said, picking me up and taking me out into the kitchen where Aunty Mary and Aunty Alice were finishing off the final preparations.

Uncle Tom came in after looking around Uncle Will's garden. "You've got some lovely sweet peas and the most enormous marrows, Will," he said. "Are you going to enter them in the village show?"

"Well, I was thinking about it," said Uncle Will.

"Stop talking about gardening, we're here to celebrate," said Aunty Mary.

"You're right, Mary. How is my lovely Victoria?" he said, turning to his niece.

"All right, Uncle Tom. Just worried with my exams coming up," she said.

"No need to worry, you'll pass with flying colours," he reassured.

Aunty Alice gestured for us all to sit at the table. I squeezed between her and Mum and had a lovely view of Farmer Allen with his sheep dogs in a field rounding up the sheep. Uncle Will began telling us how one of the dogs had recently won an award at the local sheep dog trials.

"It's nice to have you all here to celebrate a special occasion," began Aunty Alice, not wanting any further talk of Farmer Allen or his dogs.

"Yes! We're engaged!" Victoria blurted out, thrusting her hand forward, drawing everyone's attention to her sparkling engagement ring. I looked in amazement at the way it sparkled.

"It's exquisite," gasped Mum, as Tim got up for a closer inspection.

"Such flawless diamonds and they're brilliantly cut," he said.

"I should hope so. It cost enough – only the best for Victoria," said Edward.

Victoria blushed.

"We're planning our wedding for August," continued Edward. "We don't want a long engagement seeing we are hoping to take up teaching posts in September."

Victoria turned to me. "Would you be a bridesmaid at my wedding, Christine?"

"You'll have a lovely dress to wear," added Edward.

I didn't need any persuading, especially when Aunty Alice told me that Victoria's cousins, Ann and Barbara, would be bridesmaids too.

"I can't wait to be a bridesmaid," I said, imagining fairytale princesses.

"Well that's settled then," said Victoria, before giving me a hug.

We ate and discussed the reception, which Aunty Alice hoped could be held at The Jolly Miller. "We'll make sure Victoria and Edward have a wonderful reception. Could Hugh make the wedding cake?" asked Aunty Mary, referring to Uncle Will's brother who was a baker in the village.

"Yes, that's been sorted," nodded Aunty Alice looking very pleased.

"Gosh, it's getting dark already." Uncle Will stood up and walked over to a switch on the wall. I was surprised when he pressed it and a light came on.

"It's an electric light, Christine," explained Mum.

"I'm so glad we had electricity brought in. It makes such a difference, Ruby," said Aunty Alice.

"I'm sure it must," said Mum wistfully.

The grown-ups carried on chatting and I wandered into the hall to see Lassie. Before long it was time to go and we made our way to Uncle Tom's taxi. Uncle Will followed us out of the bungalow, shining his torch on the ground, and Sam took my hand so I didn't slip.

"A nice night," said Dad. "It's almost a full moon."

"See the man in the moon, Christine?" asked Sam, pointing. "If you look up at the moon, you can see the shape of a man's face."

I looked harder at the moon and thought I could make out the shape of a man. "I've seen the man in the moon!" I shouted out excitedly, and everyone chuckled in amusement.

* * *

Aunty Alice arrived early the following Wednesday to take me to the dressmakers for my bridesmaid dress fitting. She told Mum the good news that Edward had inherited some money and could buy him and Victoria a house.

"What a brilliant start for them both," said Mum. "I must go into town and buy them a wedding present."

"Make sure you buy them something decent, Ruby," said Aunty Alice. "Nothing cheap."

"I'll do my best," said Mum, sounding a bit worried.

I was just four years old at the time, but knew money was tight. Aunty Alice didn't want Victoria's new in-laws to consider us poor relations. I think it must have put Mum under pressure to keep up with the Joneses.

We got on the bus and went to dressmaker Mrs May's house. It was smartly painted in light blue with a dark blue door. Mrs May welcomed us with tea, then went to get her tape measure. She told Aunty Alice that Victoria's dress was almost complete and if she wanted, she could sneak a peek. I stood as still as I could while being measured and listened as the adults discussed the bridesmaids' dresses. They were to be satin, pale pink, with a bow at the back. I would be wearing white satin shoes, white lace gloves and a tiara decorated with pretty pink rosebuds.

"It sounds as if it will be a fairytale wedding," said Mum.

When the measuring was done, we went to see Victoria's dress. I was spellbound when Mrs May removed the cover.

"It looks like the dress Cinderella wore at the village pantomime, Mummy, but even better than that!" I gasped.

Mum agreed it was the most beautiful wedding dress she'd ever seen. "This will be the best wedding this village has seen in a while," she said.

It felt as if I was walking on clouds going home. When we got home, I took the Irish doll Sam had given me into the garden. "It's a nice day, Irene, be good for Mummy," I said as I pushed my doll's pram down the path. I fancied some strawberries so made my way to the bottom of the garden where father kept his strawberry patch. My mouth was watering and I was looking forward to eating them, when I saw Charlie the rooster. He was standing in the way, stopping me from reaching the strawberries. I was struck with fear as only the previous week Mum had told me to keep away from him.

"He's a nasty old devil and he has sharp spurs," she'd warned me.

Before I had chance to escape, Charlie spotted me. He fixed me with his beady eyes and puffed up his feathers, making him look twice as big and twice as scary. I dropped the doll's pram and ran as fast as I could back up the path, screaming for my mother, with Charlie in close pursuit. My heart pounded. I slipped and within seconds Charlie was standing over me flapping his wings, ready to attack. By this time Mum had heard my screams and raced from the cottage with a broom and began clouting Charlie. He didn't go easily and started to attack Mum. It was only when she gave him a blow that sent him flying, did he give up and retreat. It was an enormous relief when Mum picked me up and carried me inside. As we walked in, Tim stepped out of the house laughing. It wasn't until she locked the door and I felt safe that I started sobbing with relief. My knee was bleeding where I'd fallen.

"I'll clean you up and put a plaster on then I'll kiss it better," said Mum. "And I won't let Charlie chase you again."

When Dad arrived home, Mum told him what had happened and insisted in no uncertain terms that Charlie had to go.

"My poor girl," he said, picking me up.

"This is Tim's fault, always teasing him," said Mum. "He has made Charlie too dangerous to keep."

She was annoyed and during tea the following Sunday Dad explained that Charlie was gone. "That rooster was always trouble," said Tim.

"He would have been all right if you hadn't teased him," said Mum angrily.

There was a glint in Tim's eye. "Not me, Mother," he said.

"I know what goes on here," she said.

Tim began rocking backwards and forwards on the legs of his chair and looked rather sheepish.

"I didn't know the old bugger would chase Christine," he said. "He wouldn't have managed to get out of his pen if you'd shut the gate."

"How dare you try to put the blame on your mother?" said Dad sharply. "And stop swearing. We don't want Christine hearing words like that."

Tim apologised, then left the table and went out.

* * *

In the evenings, I would watch Mum and Dad clearing away the dishes and lit the oil lamps.

"Why haven't we got electric lights like Aunty Alice?" I asked one evening.

"It would cost too much to run a power cable from our nearest neighbour who has had electricity installed," said Dad.

Mum joined the conversation. "It's all right for Aunty Alice and Uncle Will, they own their bungalow, but we only rent Fir Tree Cottage. But we don't care about having electricity, we like it here."

"I like living here too," I said.

"It's family that matters most, Christine," said Mum as she pulled me close. "As long as we have each other, that's all that matters to us."

I knew even then that my parents weren't well off. Dad worked hard at the china clay clay works, but, if it weren't for Mum's raring of geese, turkeys, ducks and chickens, we wouldn't have much money at all.

A week later, Sam came home as pleased as punch having passed his driving test. "I'll hire a car and take you all out," he announced. "Anyone for a day at the seaside?" he laughed.

"Yes, Sam!" I squealed, running over to hug him.

* * *

The day of the beach trip dawned and the sun was shining. As we sat down for breakfast, I noted that the family was in a good mood. Mum was sitting with Tim, as ever. Later I would wonder if it was her watchful affection turned him into a Mummy's boy. Before the war, Tim had been hospitalised for a long time with what they thought was TB. "Some nurses were dreadful with him, the poor little mite," Mum would tell anyone who would listen. Once he was out, Mum made sure he never left her side.

Sam was singing, "In Dublin's fair city, where the girls are so pretty, I first set my eyes on sweet Molly Malone..." His dark brown hair had had a fresh cut in a slicked back style. His aftershave would fill a room when he walked in. "And that was the end of sweet Molly..." He finished the song with a wink at me. He had been singing this ever since he had been to Dublin. I enjoyed listening to him sing while eating my breakfast as Mum packed sandwiches and filled flasks with tea. Dad carried the picnic basket out and put it in the boot of the car. Sam got in the driver's seat and Tim got in beside him. I sat between my parents in the back.

"That's where I work, Christine," said Dad as we passed the clay works. I stood up on the back seat and peered out of the window. It struck me that the clay works looked much bigger now than it did from a distance.

"It's so big," I said. "Do you like working there, Daddy?"

"Well, I don't know about liking it, love, but it earns a living," he said, giving me a hug. We left the clay works behind and headed towards the coast.

This was the first time I'd seen the sea – at least I don't remember seeing it before – and as we started down towards the beach Mum spotted some lovely properties.

"Look at these beautiful houses, Jack, wouldn't it be lovely to live here?"

"We'd never afford a house like that, they must cost a fortune," he replied.

"We could, Jack. If I managed to win the football pools," she said.

"I'm not holding out much hope of that."

"Well, you never know. It's nice to dream."

"Someone has to win, Mother," Sam added encouragingly.

Once we got to the beach and started unpacking the car, Tim asked if I'd like to go looking for shells.

"I'd love that," I said, getting my bucket and spade from the boot. Sam joined us as we combed the beach, scrambling over the rocks, until my bucket was full and we decided to take it back to show our parents.

"That's a beautiful collection, Christine," said Mum. "We'll take them home to decorate the flower beds."

Sam, with his trouser legs rolled up, picked me up and twirled me around very fast, making as if he was going to throw me into the sea. Everyone laughed, but it was terrifying, as I wouldn't put it past him, so I started screaming.

"That's enough now," Dad said, noticing my distress. He got hold of me and sat me with him to calm down.

"Shall we do some paddling in the sea?" he asked. I nodded, between sobs.

"Go on then," he said.

The warm sand squished between my toes and the sun glistened on the rolling waves. It was magical.

"Jump over the waves, Christine," said Dad, grabbing my hand. I was glad he had hold of me when a big wave came in and almost knocked me over. I laughed with excitement.

When we finished our picnic lunch, Sam and Tim went for a swim while Dad helped me build a sandcastle. As the sun started to fade, we made our way home and Sam started hurrying around, packing his kit. Mum gave him a saffron cake she'd made him to take to the RAF base.

"Thanks, Mum, what would I do without you?" he said, planting a kiss on her cheek. I was always sad to see Sam leave.

Dad carried me to bed and tucked me in, reading me my favourite story about Cinderella marrying the prince. Sometimes he would finish the story before I was tired enough to fall asleep and I would try to make him stay a little longer.

"Why do you have a bald head, Dad?" I would ask with a serious face.

He would giggle. "Your mother patted me on the head too much when I was young."

That night I fell asleep quickly though, hoping to dream of my wonderful time on the beach.

The next day Aunty Alice was coming with my bridesmaid's dress. I was so excited, looking out the window for her to arrive. When she came and unpacked my dress, made of such beautiful pink satin and covered in lace, I was elated. It fit like a glove, as did my shoes.

"You look like a real fairy princess now, Christine," Mum told me proudly. Aunty Alice took my dress home with her when it was time to leave.

"We want it looking nice for Saturday," she said as she kissed me goodbye.

On the Friday evening, Sam came home with a fantastic car he'd hired. As he stepped out of it, he looked resplendent in his airforce uniform. As we were all standing around admiring it, Tim walked around the corner having caught the bus home from town.

"Gosh, I knew you were hiring a car, but not one as good as this," he gasped. "How much did it set you back?"

Sam laughed. "Edward's family are well off, so we need to make the right impression," he replied.

"Come on, boys, I've got a meal ready," said Mum.

"Good for you, Mum, you certainly know how to spoil us," said Sam. "I've been waiting for the taste of your cooking all week."

"I've made a special meal with green beans, carrots and peas."

"Garden peas?" said Sam. "Christine hasn't eaten them all, then?"

"No, Christine is a good girl. Stop teasing her, Sam!"

Sam laughed. "Come on, Mum, it's only a joke. Christine needs to get used to having her leg pulled."

After dinner Sam and Tim went out for a drive. I'd been playing mud pies and was still caked in the stuff. Dad brought the tin bath in from the washhouse, which was a stone building with a corrugated tin roof, and Mum filled the tub before washing me with lovely scented soap.

Chapter Three

IT WAS SAM'S singing that woke me the following morning, but as soon as my eyes were open, I remembered it was bridesmaid day. I jumped out of bed and ran downstairs.

"Hello bridesmaid!" Dad greeted me.

Mum offered me breakfast, but I was too excited to eat. Dad suggested milk sops, saying he'd loved them as a boy. I wanted to be like him, so I said I'd try the dish of bread soaked in warm milk with sugar sprinkled on top.

As I got ready, I told Mum how it was Sam's singing that had woken me.

"He's so excited, you'd think he was getting married," she said.

"I hope I can be a bridesmaid at Sam's wedding, Mummy," I said.

"I expect you will have to wait a long time for that, Christine," she said.

Tim was waiting outside with Dad, both looking their

smartest. Tim was often taken for a girl, on account of his brown, long ringlets and pale complexion, and that day for the first time I fully understood why – there was an angelic look about him.

Sam took me up to Aunty Alice's to travel with the bridal party.

"Your carriage awaits you, princess," he said as he opened the shiny door. Sam had been polishing the car for hours. When we were driving through the village, Sam waved at some boys he knew. "Gosh, did you see the way they looked at me, Christine?" he asked. "They couldn't believe their eyes, seeing me driving a smart car like this."

The scent of roses was exhilarating as we entered Aunty Alice's bungalow. "We've only just had the flowers delivered. Aren't they lovely?" said Barbara. "Come on then. Aunty Alice is waiting to put your bridesmaid's dress on."

I followed Barbara through to one of the bedrooms. I could see that Aunty Alice was already helping Ann. She had her dress on and was looking really beautiful. I stood watching Aunty Alice as she put on Ann's tiara. I couldn't wait to wear mine. I could hear giggles coming from Victoria's bedroom where she was getting ready.

Soon I was in my dress and Aunty Alice turned me so I could look in the mirror. I couldn't believe my eyes. Was that really my reflection looking back at me?

"Now for the tiara," said Aunty Alice, undoing the ribbons in my curly hair. It was every bit as wonderful as I'd hoped. I smiled with pleasure as Barbara brought over my beautiful white satin shoes.

I could hear Victoria giggling again as her friend Doreen came out of her room.

"Has anyone got something that Victoria can borrow?" she asked.

"Victoria can borrow my gold cross," said Ann, and took it off.

"Thanks, Ann. Now we need something blue."

I remembered I had worn my blue ribbons. "Victoria can have my blue ribbons," I said, delighted to help.

"That's an excellent idea, Christine," smiled Doreen. "She can thread the blue ribbons through her garter."

"We need something old now," said Doreen, looking at Aunty Alice.

"I've got just the thing – Victoria's grandmother's bracelet," said Aunty Alice going to her jewellery box. Doreen thanked her and returned to Victoria.

"There is one thing left to do," said Aunty Alice to Uncle Will.

"What's that?"

"You need a silver sixpence to slip into Victoria's shoe."

Uncle Will scratched his head in bewilderment and went to the jar where he kept his change. "Will this one do?" he asked. Aunty Alice nodded.

"It's for good luck and prosperity. Slip it into her shoe before going down the aisle," she whispered.

Victoria's door opened and we caught our first glimpse of the bride. She looked beautiful and it was our job to carry the train on her dress to keep it off the ground. We drove to the church and I walked proudly behind Victoria through the gates and along the pathway. As we got closer to the door and we heard the first notes strike up from the organ, I suddenly felt in awe of my surroundings and overwhelmed by the sanctity and significance of the occasion. Uncle Will glanced at Victoria and he took her arm. It was plain for all to see how proud he was of his daughter. The church was full and everyone was looking at us as we walked down the aisle. I looked for my parents and was pleased when I spotted them near the front, sitting with my brothers. Mum looked magnificent in a lilac dress, Sam was wearing his RAF uniform, and Dad and Tim looked smart in their best suits.

When the ceremony was over, I followed Victoria and Edward back down the aisle. The sun was shining and people started throwing rice and brightly coloured confetti. Aunty Alice busied herself organising the photographs and called to me. "Come on, Christine, we want to take one of you with your two brothers."

Mum and Dad were pleased that they were going to have a lovely picture of the three of us for the sideboard.

We were soon off to The Jolly Miller, which was beautifully decorated with pink and white balloons and colourful garlands. The tables looked amazing, set out with starch white cloths and gleaming silver cutlery. I felt my mouth water as I spotted the beautifully iced four-tiered wedding cake, which took pride of place on the centre table. We took our places for the toast. As bridesmaids, Ann, Barbara and I were each given a beautiful silver bracelet. I was thrilled to receive such a wonderful gift.

We all thanked Victoria and Edward and I ran over to show

my parents.

"Your girls are very pretty today," Aunt Mary said to Mum, looking mischievously at Tim and me.

"I'm a boy," Tim protested, indignantly, pulling up his overcoat. "Look, I'm wearing trousers." Everyone laughed and Aunt Mary winked at me.

Music filled the air and Aunty Mary called for Victoria and Edward to take the first dance. We all followed, keen to see them dancing for the first time as a married couple. Then the dance floor filled up and everyone danced the night away until it was time for Victoria and Edward to leave for their honeymoon in the Lake District. While everyone was wishing them well, I noticed Tim and Sam sneaking away and wondered what they were up to. We followed the newlyweds out to the car park wanting to wave them goodbye as Uncle Tom opened the taxi door for them to get in.

"Look at the old boots and tin cans tied to the bumper of the car, Mummy," I said. "Why has someone done that?"

"It's a tradition, Christine," said Mum, and started to laugh. Everyone else was smiling too and I suddenly realised that Sam and Tim were the culprits. I spotted them looking out of the window, both grinning like Cheshire cats.

"Best wishes for a very happy married life!" I heard someone shout as the taxi pulled out of the car park. I looked on in amusement as the tin cans rattled and clanged on the cobbles, and the old boots started swinging from side to side. Victoria looked out of the back window and gave us one last wave. I could not help feeling a bit sad watching her go, and knew I would not see much of her now that she was leaving Cornwall. Mum said they were going to Luton, where Victoria's new in-laws lived and where she and her new husband had obtained teaching jobs.

"Don't feel sad, Christine," said Dad. "Victoria will come down to see you when she's on holiday."

As we got ready to go home Aunty Alice gave us our wedding cake, which cheered me up. Back home at Fir Tree, we all had a cup of tea and our slice of wedding cake. Dad carried me upstairs to bed, with Mum following. She got me undressed and hung my beautiful bridesmaid's dress in the wardrobe. As soon as my head hit the pillow, I was asleep.

Chapter Four

"COME ON, CHRISTINE, we're going out"

I opened my eyes to the sound of my mother's voice. The sun shone through a gap in the curtain.

"Time for breakfast, Christine," she called again. I could smell bacon and knew Mum was doing a cooked breakfast, something she only did at weekends or on special occasions. I climbed out of bed and ran downstairs still in my nightdress. Sam was sat at the table and Mum was at the Cornish range cooker.

"Morning, Sam. Morning, Mummy. Are we going to the beach?" I asked. Very much wanting Dad to buy me a kite so I could fly it on the beach.

"No, we're going to the fruit farm to pick plums," said Mum. "I want to make plum jam."

"Yummy!" I said, thinking of bread, butter and jam.

"I hope so. Now eat your breakfast while it's hot."

I tucked into my bacon, sausage, egg and fried bread.

"Can you do me a strong tea please, Mum?" asked Sam.

She stirred the teapot vigorously and poured one out for Sam. "There you go," she said. "You can stand your spoon up in that. I don't know how you drink it."

Sam laughed. "A strong cuppa and some burnt toast for me," he said, reaching for another slice.

"Yes, your father must have been thinking of you earlier when he made the toast. It's black."

Sam spread the charred bread with butter just as Tim came in from feeding the turkeys, followed by Dad with a basket of eggs.

"Morning, Christine," said Tim and Dad together.

I had a mouthful of food and mumbled a good morning. Sam scoffed the last of his toast, swigged his tea and pushed his chair backwards. "We'd better get ready," he said.

I went upstairs with Mum and was pleased to be able to show her I could get myself dressed. She was delighted as it would help me when I started school and we had PE.

It was decided that we would go to Tamar Farm, and we squeezed into the car with all the plastic tubs for the plums.

"I want a car like this when I pass my test," said Tim.

"I doubt you'll afford a car like this," Sam retorted.

"I've started saving actually."

"Perhaps we could pool our money and buy a family car," suggested Dad.

"Good idea," said Mum.

"It would be cheaper in the long run," said Sam.

"You keep on saving then, Tim," said Dad, patting him on the back.

"Do you think Goldilocks and the three bears live in these

woods, Daddy?" I asked, gazing through the window.

"They might do, Christine," he said.

"Can we stop and see them?"

"Not today, we don't have time."

We had a lovely day picking plums. Tim asked me to taste the first one to see if they were sweet enough, then I sat in the orchard watching the sun twinkle through the leaves as my brothers raced up and down the ladder to get the best fruit. Eventually it was decided we had enough plums, so weighed and paid and made our way home. I was tired and snuggled into my mother on the journey back before Dad carried me into the cottage.

"Who wants chicken broth?" asked Mum.

We all did, and Sam just had time before he had to make his way back to base. We sat and watched as our mother heated the broth. When we'd eaten, Sam went upstairs to get his uniform.

"Come here, son," Mum said to Sam, putting her cheek out for a kiss.

"Me too, give me a kiss too, Sam!" I said, running over to him. He picked me up and kissed me.

"Be good, Christine," he said. "Help Mummy make the jam."

"I will."

With Sam gone, it was time for bed. "Apples and pears and up the stairs," said Mum, holding my hand and encouraging me up the stairs as I attempted to count them. "Goodnight, Christine dear," she said. "Sweet dreams."

* * *

The happy warble of a blackbird woke me the next morning. I got up and opened the curtains. The countryside was spread before me, green grass and golden corn. I looked into the distance at the clay hills. When it rained, they looked dull and bleak, but with the sun casting its rays upon the white sand, with its high quartz content, they positively sparkled.

Mum came into my room with a jug of warm water that she put on the wash stand. "I'll get myself washed and dressed today, Mummy," I said.

"Good girl," she said. "You'll be starting school next week."

"Will I Mummy?" I could feel butterflies in my tummy. I wanted to go to school so that I could play with other children, but I was nervous.

"Yes, and the postman just arrived with a parcel actually. I think it must be your new school clothes that I ordered from the catalogue. You can try them on after we've fed the animals."

That particular morning as we walked to the field where the turkeys were, I could smell honeysuckle growing on the hedge and was fascinated by the bumble bees buzzing in and out of the flowers. Mum explained how they made honey. On the way back we saw our neighbour Mrs Hendy picking blackberries from the hedge.

"My girls' love apple and blackberry pie," she told us. "So I thought I'd give them a treat tonight. They'll enjoy that after having been in an office all day."

"Lovely idea," said Mum. "The blackberries have been so plentiful, even now in late September."

"I hear you're starting school, Christine?" said Mrs Hendy

looking at me.

"Yes, I can't wait," I said, jiggling about in excitement.

"She's a bit late starting isn't she, Ruby?" Mrs Hendy asked.

"Yes, my sister Maggie paid a visit all the way from South Africa," Mum replied. "We asked if Christine could start later so that she could see her."

"So the school agreed. That was nice of them," Mrs Hendy commented.

After lunch I put on my new uniform – a bottle-green pleated skirt, white blouse and bottle-green cardigan.

"You look really grown up, just like a proper school girl," said Mum. When Dad arrived home from early shift, I couldn't wait to show him.

"Doesn't she look smart, Jack?" said Mum. "You won't be able to call her your baby anymore."

"No I won't, she's a big girl now," Dad agreed smiling.

He came inside the cottage and I showed him my new red coat with velvet trim collar and matching hat, also from the catalogue. Dad was very impressed, as was Tim when he came home later.

"You look like Red Riding Hood!" he laughed. "You'd better watch out that the Big Bad Wolf doesn't get you."

* * *

"Do you think the other children will like me, Mummy?" I asked. My first day at school was finally here and I was worried.

She gave me a reassuring hug. "Of course they will, Christine. By the end of the day you'll have too many friends to count."

It was a chilly day so Mum said I could wear my new coat. She took her bicycle out of the shed and lifted me into the child's seat on the back. As we approached the school, I could hear children's voices, playing and laughing.

"What's that game they're playing, Mummy?" I asked, intrigued to see girls jumping over chalk squares drawn on the playground floor.

"It's hopscotch, Christine. It's great fun. I used to play it with Aunty Alice when I was a girl."

Mum lifted me out of the seat and took me into the playground. She knew the school well as both my brothers had gone there. "Let's find your teacher," she said.

We entered a classroom where a nice lady teacher came over. "Hello," she said to my mum, "I've been expecting you and Christine."

My mother looked sad. "I'll miss my little companion helping me feed the chickens and turkeys."

The teacher smiled. "Christine, my name is Miss Penrose. I'm pleased to have you joining my class. Shall I show you where to hang your coat and hat?"

Miss Penrose led my mother and I to the cloakroom and to a coat peg that had my name above it. "This is your coat peg, Christine. I've written your name above it so you can find it."

I felt very pleased. Mum helped me take my coat and hat off and hang them up, then walked me back to the classroom and paid for my school dinners. "I'll pay weekly," she told Miss Penrose.

Looking back, it was clear that my mother was reluctant to leave me. Miss Penrose was no doubt used to this and told her not to worry, that she would look after me.

"I'll see you at half-past-three," Mum told me. I felt upset as she walked away, but then the bell rang and it was time for me to take a seat and for the register to be called. I got the hang of it and when it was my turn, I found myself answering, "Yes, Miss," like all the others. A couple of the girls smiled at me, and I smiled back, thinking how much I wanted them to like me. Miss Penrose spoke to the girl sitting next to me. "Sheila, could you please look after Christine and show her around at playtime?"

"Yes, Miss." Sheila smiled at me and I smiled back. Then Miss Penrose handed out picture books. When I opened the first page I could see an apple and the words "A is for Apple", and I felt glad my mother had been teaching me the alphabet. After the lesson we did some drawing, then Miss Penrose handed everyone a small bottle of milk with a straw.

The bell rang signalling the end of the morning classes. Sheila took me to the canteen where I queued up with her for dinner. She told me her eldest brother had been in the same class as Sam, which made me feel at ease. Sheila introduced me to two other girls, Maureen and Hazel. After we'd finished eating we all went out in the playground.

"Do you want to have a go at skipping, Christine?" Sheila asked when Hazel produced her skipping rope. I didn't feel ready but held the rope as Hazel and Sheila took turns to skip. An afternoon of learning our letters was followed by Miss Penrose reading the story of The Elves and the Shoemaker.

Time flew by very quickly, and before I knew, I saw my mother at the window. It was home time already.

"I've made new friends, Mummy!" I said.

"I'm so pleased! I knew you would."

Mum and I got on the bike and sailed down the hill to Fir Tree Cottage. It had been a very good day at school and I couldn't wait to go back.

Chapter Five

I SETTLED INTO school well and enjoyed most of my lessons. Sheila and I were inseparable, and we played with Maureen and Hazel at break time. A ripple of excitement spread through the class the day Miss Penrose produced paper chains to decorate our class in time for our Christmas party.

One Saturday before Christmas, Aunty Alice and my mother took me into St Austell for some Christmas shopping.

"I've heard that Father Christmas is in town. Do you want to see him?" asked Aunty Alice. I was thrilled with the idea.

"We'll go there first," said Mum, "before we get loaded down with shopping."

We got off the bus and followed Aunty Alice into a brightly decorated department store. We made our way upstairs to Father Christmas's Grotto. This was the first time I'd got to see Father Christmas and was feeling very excited. I couldn't believe my eyes. The grotto was far better than I could ever have imagined. There was a woodland glen with a wishing well and beautifully made toy fairies, elves and gnomes.

"Would you like to make a wish, Christine?" asked Aunty Alice, handing me a penny which I threw into the well. I closed my eyes and wished for a large painting box for Christmas.

It really was an incredible grotto, with more than one room, each seemingly more amazing than the last. All of them were a winter wonderland with sparkling white walls and icicles hanging from the ceiling. In another room I was completely enthralled by the sight of Sleeping Beauty and Snow White, and when I saw the life-sized Cinderella with a pumpkin coach and handsome Prince Charming, I gasped and stood dead still, unable to move.

"Come on, Christine" said Mum finally. "Don't you want to see Father Christmas?" I did want to see Father Christmas and get a present. As I turned the corner, I caught a glimpse of him. I thought he looked a bit scary in his bright red suit and his white beard. Mum pushed me towards him but I stepped backwards, feeling unsure. "Come over and see Father Christmas, he wants to give you a present," she said taking me by the hand.

Father Christmas delved into his sack and encouraged me over. An assistant approached my mother. "Would you like to have her photo taken sitting on Father Christmas's knee?"

"Yes please," she said. "Her father would love to see that."

I was getting used to Father Christmas and his jolly smile, so I sat on his knee and he asked me what I wanted for Christmas.

"A big box of paints please," I said.

"I'll see what I can do," he said, winking at my mother.

"Smile for the camera, Christine, just like when you were a

bridesmaid," prompted Aunty Alice. The thought of being a bridesmaid made me smile and the photograph was taken.

"That's a good girl," said Father Christmas, handing me my present. I tore the paper open and was delighted to find a magic drawing pad. It was just what I wanted and I loved the way I could write on the pad, wipe it, and start drawing another picture.

We all said thank you for the lovely gift and waved goodbye to Father Christmas.

"Don't forget! I'll be coming down your chimney on Christmas Eve," he said, and I left the grotto feeling very excited.

As we were leaving the shop, my mother spotted some lovely party dresses and held one up. It was powder-blue seersucker.

"Try on this lovely dress, Christine" she said, calling me over and leading me to the changing room.

"It's lovely," said Aunty Alice. "Her white bridesmaid's shoes would look nice with it."

I felt like Cinderella when I looked in the mirror. "Will you buy it for me, Mummy, please?" I begged.

"Yes, I'm sure your father won't mind. We've sold a lot of turkeys."

"You're a lucky girl, Christine," said Aunty Alice as we left the shop. I knew she was right. I felt like the luckiest girl in the world. I couldn't wait to show my father and my brothers. And they all agreed it was perfect.

The next week it was the carol service and Miss Penrose asked me to recite Twinkle, Twinkle Little Star. I was sure I was too shy but when it came to it, I plucked up the courage and spoke as loudly as I could, my eyes fixed on my parents sitting in the front row.

The service was wonderful and I felt so proud when I heard my parents and Aunty Alice singing Hark the Herald Angels Sing. I loved hearing Aunty Alice's sweet soprano voice, with her beautiful celestial tones, rising above the others. At the end of the service the headmaster said a few words and wished everyone a Merry Christmas. I gave Aunty Alice a big hug before she left, and caught hold of my parents' hands as we walked back to Fir Tree Cottage, with both my mum and dad telling me how proud they were of me and that I'd done really well.

I got to wear my seersucker dress at the school Christmas party the following day. One of the boys said I looked like a fairy, which pleased me no end. It was a magical occasion. At lunchtime I felt far too excited to eat, with my mind on party cakes and jellies.

When we returned later to our classroom the desks had been put together and covered with wonderful red and green tablecloths, all very festive with each place decorated with a cracker. My mouth started watering when I saw the plates of sandwiches, cakes, fancies, chocolate fingers and lovely jellies. I had my eye on a fancy cake topped with white and pink icing and just couldn't wait to taste it. We played games that were new to me, such as Pass the Parcel and Postman's Knock. Miss Penrose gave us each a gift and we wished each other a happy Christmas holiday.

* * *

I was helping Mum make scones, saffron buns and Christmas

pudding when my father came home with a Christmas tree. I felt excited as he stood it in the corner for us to decorate with brightly coloured balls and gold and silver tinsel. We put Christmas crackers on the branches to the sound of carols playing on the radio. I watched as Dad put holly sprigs and mistletoe around the room.

"You had better go to bed early tonight and get to sleep, or Father Christmas won't come down your chimney," Mum told me on Christmas Eve.

I had butterflies in my tummy as I got ready for bed – I didn't want to miss him. When I woke up and saw a big sack of gifts at the bottom of my bed, I shouted, "Mummy! Daddy! Father Christmas has been!" and ran into their bedroom. "Look at this great big box of paints, Mummy. It's enormous."

"Father Christmas has been good to you," Dad told me, looking at the dolls, Snap cards, Snakes-and-Ladders and painting and drawing books I'd received, along with a big selection box of chocolates.

"Father Christmas must think you're a very good girl," said Mum. "And look, there's a gift from Aunty Alice and Uncle Will here too."

I tore off the paper. It was a scarf and glove set.

"That will keep you warm on the way to school," said Mum.

"Yes, but I like toys best," I said, making Dad chuckle.

"Get dressed, Christine," said Mum. "You can come downstairs and play while I prepare the turkey."

I got dressed and followed her downstairs. Sam and Tim came down soon after eyeing my presents.

"You are lucky, he didn't used to bring us this much," said Tim. "Fancy a game of Snap?"

"Yes please," I said.

Snap was my favourite although I always felt sure Tim was cheating. We went on to play Snakes-and-Ladders until it was time for Christmas lunch. That Christmas, as I got close to winning against Tim, he whacked the board, making the pieces fly up in the air. "You brat!" he hissed through gritted teeth. I stared at him and quickly left the room after.

The turkey was delicious. Mum assured us that she had saved the best bird for our own meal.

"You're a champion at rearing turkeys, Ruby," said Dad.

She blushed. "Don't flatter me, Jack."

* * *

Christmas came and went too fast. Sam returned to his RAF base and Tim went back to work. I was looking forward to seeing my friends at school and hearing what Father Christmas brought them.

The first day back was exciting. It was so cold that Miss Penrose warmed our milk for us. I wore my scarf and gloves in the playground, glad for Aunty Alice's gift. Later we overheard the teacher saying it was cold enough for snow.

When the school bell rang and it was time to go home, I got my coat and hat and made my way to the gate keen to see Mum. It was a shock to find that she wasn't there waiting. This had never happened to me before. I watched as the other children were collected, until I was, before long, standing there alone. I knew something must be wrong, and just as I was about to cry, I saw Mrs Hendy hurrying towards me.

"Christine!" she said, breathless. "Your mother's been taken ill, so I've come to fetch you. I'll just go and explain to your teacher."

As we walked home, I asked Mrs Hendy, "What's happened to Mummy?"

"I don't know, Christine," she said. "She's lying on the sofa. I've sent Jim up to the clay works to fetch your father. He'll get the doctor."

Chapter Six

THE SIGHT OF my mother when I walked through the door hit me like a ton of bricks. She tried speaking but I could barely understand her. Crouching down beside her, I managed to make out the words.

"I can't move down one side," she said.

Panic coursed through me as Mrs Hendy busied about making me eggs for tea. I couldn't eat, and sat staring at Mum, straining for the sound of my father's motorbike.

When he arrived, he knelt down beside my mother and told Mrs Hendy that Dr Davis was on her way. I sat on the floor beside the sofa holding Mum's hand.

When the doctor arrived, my father told me to go upstairs and play. I sat at the top of the stairs and listened to the low, urgent voices.

"I'll give you a prescription, Jack. Go and get it right away," said Dr Davis. "I'll wait here with Christine and Ruby. Hurry, you must catch the chemist before he closes."

When Dad returned, Dr Davis gave him instructions about the medicine and said she'd be back in the morning. "Don't leave Ruby on her own," she said.

My father thanked the doctor and said he would arrange for time off work. When she had gone, I slowly crept downstairs. Dad was trying to make Mum more comfortable on the sofa. "I think you are best to stay on the sofa for a while, Ruby, while I get the tea," he told her. Mum gave him a half smile and I could see that only one side of her face was working. I heard the gate hinge creak and knew it was Tim. He came in looking cheerful, but when he saw Mum, his face went white.

"What's wrong with mother?" he asked.

"We're not sure at the moment, but the Doctor's saying she might have had a stroke." My father's voice cracked with emotion.

"A stroke!" Tim just stood there, staring at our mother.

"Yes. After tea I need you to go up to Mill Hill and tell Aunty Alice. I'll take a week off and hopefully she can help with Christine."

After tea Tim went off and Dad carried Mum upstairs to the bedroom. I went up after a while and climbed on the bed to give her a cuddle.

"Your mother is feeling too ill for a cuddle, Christine. She needs to rest," said Dad. "I need you to be a big girl now, so can you do your dad a favour, and get yourself ready for bed?"

I felt desperately sad. "All right, Daddy," I said. It seemed like things would never be the same again and I cried myself to sleep.

A crushing sorrow in my heart told me the following

morning that I had not been dreaming. My mother was seriously ill. Aunty Alice arrived, followed by Dr Davis. When she left I heard Dad and Aunty Alice talking as I sat on the floor of the living room pretending to play. "It doesn't sound very good, Jack," said Aunty Alice. "Dr Davis thinks Ruby should improve, but nothing is certain."

"I know," he said. "I'll have to get rid of the poultry. I'll be sad to see the turkeys go but they were very much Ruby's thing and she's too ill to look after them."

"That's a wise decision, Jack. You'll have enough to do."

Alice and my father made arrangements regarding the turkeys, and he left to see if a teacher from my school could take me and collect me each day as she passed.

Aunty Alice came into the living room. "I thought you might like a beaker of milk, Christine," she said, handing it to me. "I know you have milk at school."

"Thank you," I said. "Is it all right for me to see Mummy?"

Aunty Alice put her arm around me. "Your mother is asleep Christine, so not yet. Just play quietly and try not to wake her."

"When will Mummy be better?"

"We don't know, Christine. She needs a lot of rest."

Dad came home sometime later. He had managed to offload the turkeys and Mrs Hendy offered to get me ready each morning. A teacher called Miss Truscott had agreed to drive me to and from school, and Aunty Alice said she would come daily to make my tea.

I listened to Aunty Alice and Dad as I played with my dolls.

"Make sure you're good for Miss Truscott, it's so kind of

her," said Dad.

"I will be good, Daddy."

"I know you will," he said. "Things are a bit difficult for us now."

Aunty Alice came downstairs and put her coat on. "Ruby is still sleeping," she told Dad before turning to me. "I'll see you again tomorrow, Christine."

I didn't want her to leave and clung on to her coat. "Help your father, Christine. He needs all the help he can get," she said. Then she was gone.

When Tim came home Dad made egg, bacon and chips for tea for us and soup for Mum. He updated Tim about the turkeys.

"Tough decision," said Tim. "The right thing to do. But mother will be upset when she finds out."

When it was bedtime, I went in to give her a kiss.

"Goodnight, Mummy, I love you," I said, and hoped that my words would make her better.

The next few days were a blur. Miss Truscott took me to and from school. I felt upset when we passed the empty turkey field, realising I'd never feed the turkeys with Mum again. My friends knew what had happened and they were all very kind to me. At the weekend Sam came home.

"Come here, little sister," he said, picking me up and giving me a hug. "It's a sad time for us all." He gave me some milk before Dad and Tim came home and we sat and ate. It felt awful that Mum was up there all alone while we were downstairs eating. After the meal Dad went to see her. Sam cleared the dishes and Tim went to draw water from the well.

"How did this happen?" Sam asked Tim when he came in from the garden.

"It seems mother was brushing the stairs, and she knocked her hand on the banister," Tim told him. "It sounds as if knocking her hand caused the stroke."

"I had no idea just knocking your hand could cause a stroke," said Sam.

"Mother must have been rushing around, worried about being late to collect Christine," said Tim. "I doubt she would have knocked her hand if she wasn't in such a hurry."

"The thing is, she was a lot younger when we started school," said Sam.

"It's all been too much for her, feeding the animals, cleaning the house, and having to go up to school to pick Christine up," said Tim.

There was a dark tone to his voice that made me shudder. All day I couldn't think of anything else but that I was to blame for the stroke. Even when I heard Sam say it wasn't my fault, I couldn't get the thought from my mind.

Dad came downstairs to get some soup for Mum and asked if I wanted to go up to see her. I felt relieved and followed him up the stairs.

"Sam is home and all the family are here, Ruby," he said to Mum as she smiled her half-smile that was now becoming familiar. I sat and watched as he fed her, worrying as some of the soup trickled out that it might stain her nightdress. The next day I could barely concentrate at school. Was Tim right? Was I to blame for our mother's stroke?

* * *

Over the next few weeks, I spent as much time as I was able sitting beside Mum, holding her hand and telling her about school and the games we played there. Various people took care of me and a lady called Mrs Lane came in each day to take care of Mum. Months went by and I was losing hope, until one day I came home to see Aunty Alice looking much happier.

"It looks as if your mother's getting better, Christine," she said. "The doctor's very pleased with the progress she's made."

My heart leapt with joy. "That's wonderful," I said.

"It seems that she is getting some feeling back."

A few weeks later I came home from school to find Mum downstairs sitting in her favourite chair. I rushed towards her and hugged her tightly.

"I'm glad that you're so much better, Mummy!" I said.

"It's nice to be back downstairs again," she said, kissing me on the cheek.

As the weeks went by, I was glad to see Mum slowly improving. She started making her way around the cottage, holding on to the furniture when she felt unsteady. After a while it was agreed that Aunty Alice and Mrs Lane didn't need to call every day. Mrs Lane just came three times a week to help with housework.

The summer holidays were nearly here, but first it was sports day on the final day of term. I got roped into the three-legged race with Hazel. It was hilarious, with everyone falling over onto the grass. But when the parents lined up for the egg-and-spoon race, I felt a jolt of sadness that my mother couldn't be there.

When I got home, Mum told me she had been looking forward to the holidays. "I'm never lonely with you around, Christine," she said.

"I'm glad too, Mummy," I said.

"Yes, and Aunty Alice has bought you a new ball."

She handed me a very bouncy rainbow-coloured ball. I went outside to play with it, throwing it against the wall like we did at school.

"Would you like me to make you a swing, Christine?" Dad asked one afternoon.

"I'd love that, Daddy," I replied, jumping up and down.

He grinned at my excitement. "Come on then, let's get some wood and a piece of rope out of the shed."

I followed him. "Just what I'm looking for," he said, spotting some wood and a coil of rope.

"How long will it take to make it, Daddy?"

"Not long," he said, grinning again. "Just have to plane the wood to make it smooth enough."

I watched intently as he worked. "Now all I need to do is drill a few holes to thread the rope through," he said.

"You are clever aren't you, Daddy?" I said once he'd threaded the rope through and tied the knots securely.

He smiled at me. "Not really, love, not clever enough," he said, stopping to give me a hug. "We'll tie it onto the long branch of the fir tree."

I followed, running behind him to the fir tree. "Here, try it out for size. It's not too far off the ground, is it?"

I was over the moon as I climbed onto the wooden seat. "No, it's just right, Daddy," I squealed with delight. He looked pleased to see me happy.

"I'll give you a push and see how you get on," he said, getting behind me.

I felt I could burst with happiness as the swing went higher. "I love it. Thank you, Daddy," I shouted. After a while he stopped pushing.

"Take care, mind. We don't want you falling off," he said, standing back. "It's time for me to make your Mum a cup of tea."

Moments spent on that swing make some of the most vivid memories of my childhood. I could hear a cuckoo calling, the sound echoed in the air. The air was filled with the sweet smell of honeysuckle. The beautiful pink rhododendron bush looked resplendent in bloom. From the swing, the fir tree looked enormous, like a sharp wedge into the sky.

"Daddy's made me a swing, Mummy," I told her as soon as I got in.

She held out her arms to give me a cuddle. "Yes, he was telling me," she said, giving me a hug. "Aren't you a lucky girl?" I nodded and gave her a kiss.

Chapter Seven

I'D BEEN HOME from school for about four weeks when we received a visit from the village policeman. He arrived at the cottage on his bike and I was sent out to play so I didn't hear what he was saying to my parents.

When I went back inside, Mum was crying and asked me to get her another handkerchief.

"What's wrong, Mummy?" I asked, but neither she nor my father answered.

Everyone seemed very sad and the following day I asked Aunty Alice what had happened. "We're all feeling very sad, Christine, because Uncle Tom has died and gone to heaven," she said.

I didn't know what she meant by "died" or "gone to heaven," but felt unable to ask as she started crying. I decided to ask Dad when he came home from work.

"Why are Mummy and Aunty Alice sad about Uncle Tom, Daddy?"

He looked lost for words. "Uncle Tom had a heart attack, dear," he replied.

"Aunty Alice said he's gone to heaven," I said.

"It's hard to explain," he said. "Uncle Tom had a heart attack and the doctor couldn't save him, so now he has gone up to heaven to live instead."

"Is it nice up in heaven?" I asked, not sure where it was or why he had gone there.

"I'm sure it is, love." He patted my head. "It's not something you need to worry about at your age."

I didn't go to Uncle Tom's funeral. I stayed at the pub with a lady called Maud and waited for everyone to come back for tea. People started telling lovely stories about Uncle Tom that made everyone smile. When we got home, I asked Dad why everyone was so upset that Uncle Tom had gone to heaven.

"They're upset because they'll miss Uncle Tom," he said.

"Won't we see him again, Daddy?"

"Yes, of course we will dear, when we go to heaven."

I was pleased to hear that I would see him again and returned to playing.

Tim came home a few weeks later with some good news for Mum. "I've booked driving lessons," he said. "And when I pass my test, I'll be able to take you out."

Her face lit up and Tim looked thrilled to see the sparkle coming back in her eyes. "Wait 'til I tell the old man," he said.

"Wonderful, son," said Mum. "It's nice Sam can drive, but he's away a lot."

"I'll be able to take you out for Sunday afternoon drives."

Tim's news seemed to give her the boost she needed, and she started to recover much more quickly. It wasn't long before Tim passed his test, and just a few weeks after that there was a car on the drive. Dad and Tim had saved together, and Sam put some money in the kitty too. The car was black and incredibly shiny, and I loved it. I really enjoyed the smell of the comfortable leather seats. Soon my dreams of sandcastles and paddling in the sea turned to reality as we began having weekend trips to Carlyon Bay, on the Cornish coast.

Sam had been away for some months by now, but when he eventually got leave he was chuffed to see the car. In fact, I felt he was paying more attention to the vehicle than to me. I pulled at his trouser leg to get his attention. "Do you want a whiz, Christine?" he said, and he picked me up and spun me round, then carried me inside for tea.

Some weeks later, Sam brought a friend called Larry home from the base. I couldn't understand a word he was saying and Sam had to explain to me that he was something called a "Cockney". Larry didn't pay much attention to me. He, Sam and Tim would sit by the Cornish range with a cup of tea, talking about cars, motorbikes and engines. Larry came to visit quite a lot after that.

On one occasion they were up in their rooms talking when they started whispering, which I found annoying as I couldn't hear what they were saying. Dad must have heard them whispering too and called Sam out into the garden to have a word with him on his own. I realised something was wrong when I heard them arguing, and I hid between the raspberry bushes so they wouldn't know I was there.

"Please don't be stupid, Sam." Dad sounded fraught. "For goodness sake listen to reason, don't be a fool. You'll be in serious trouble if you get caught."

"It's you who's stupid, old man," said Sam. "We won't get caught. We're too smart for that."

I had no idea what was going on but a few weeks later I woke up early and went downstairs to find Sam, Tim and Larry sitting in the living room with lots of men's shirts, sheets, blankets, towels, sweets and chocolate piled up on the table. I stared in amazement.

"Do you want a bar of chocolate, Christine?" asked Sam.

"Where did you get it from?" I asked, as he handed me a big bar.

"Don't worry your pretty little head about that," he said. "We've been late-night shopping." They all burst out laughing.

"Why did you buy all those bars of chocolate?" I asked.

"Because we know you like chocolate!" said Sam.

Father appeared, looking very shocked. "What the hell have you been up to?" he demanded.

"Don't worry, old man," said Sam. "We'll take it upstairs out of the way."

"You bloody idiots," he said. "I never thought you'd be so stupid."

"You'll never have anything if you aren't prepared to take a few chances," Sam told him.

"God helps them who help themselves," added Larry.

As the boys went upstairs, Dad told me not to say a word to

anyone as I would get the boys in trouble. Sam heard him as he was leaving the room and spoke to me sharply. "You mustn't tell anyone at school, it's no one else's business," he said. "If you do, they will come and take your chocolate bars away. You don't want that, do you?"

I could see them both looking at me expecting an answer. "No, I won't tell anyone," I promised, but I didn't really understand why.

When Sam and Larry went back to their base, Tim suggested an afternoon drive to Carlyon Bay. I didn't have to be asked twice and I raced to collect my bucket and spade from the wash house. As we drove, Mum admired the beautiful houses again. She sighed and I could see she was dreaming of sitting in one of the nice gardens.

"I think I'll have another go at the football pools, Jack," she said.

"If you want to, my dear."

When we got onto the beach, Dad reached into his bag and surprised me with a brightly-coloured kite. Tim joined in helping me hold the strings until it rose in the air to fly far above us. I noticed a crowd of children watching us admiringly as my kite was flying higher than the rest. It was such a happy day.

The next day at school, I heard something that gave me goose bumps. Two teachers were talking to each other at break time, discussing a break-in at the Co-op on Saturday night.

"A lot went," said one teacher. "Shirts, bedding and towels, in fact anything they could get their hands on, I'm told."

"Oh my, I don't know anyone around here who'd do that,"

said the other teacher.

"It's most likely strangers."

"Whoever it was had a sweet tooth. They stole loads of chocolate bars."

I thought of the chocolate bar I had eaten and felt extremely uneasy. Wasn't this too much of a coincidence? Sam and Tim wouldn't do something like that, would they? I knew I couldn't say anything.

A few days later the four of us were sat down to tea when there was a knock at the door. Dad looked nervous, and when he answered he found two burly policemen standing there. "We have a warrant to search your house," they said.

Mum tried to get up but fell right back down again as if her legs had given out beneath her. The policemen went upstairs and found all the loot in Sam's and Tim's bedrooms. They returned carrying the stolen shirts, chocolate bars and many other things. Mum looked shocked and Dad looked very worried. Tim just seemed angry he'd been caught, but was shaking and looked scared.

"We've arrested your son Sam at the airforce base," the officer informed my parents. "He's in our cells now. It seems he has been selling shirts there which he stole from the Co-op on Saturday night. Now we'll have to arrest your other son."

"No, no, not my Tim, he wouldn't do it," Mum cried out.

Dad looked very concerned and tried to comfort her.

The policeman looked at my mother and seemed genuinely concerned. "I'm sorry, my dear," he said, "but as you can see, I have searched their rooms and have found the stolen items."

I was frozen to the spot as I watched Tim being handcuffed, Mum pleading that there was some mistake. Tim didn't make a fuss, not wanting to further upset Mum. She told him she loved him and it would soon be sorted out. We listened in silence as the police car drove away.

"Jack!" said Mum. "Did you know what they were up to?"

My father looked sheepish. "I heard them talking about it, Ruby, but never thought they'd be daft enough to do it." He put his arm around her to comfort her but she was having none of it. She started to sob.

"You should have told me, Jack, I would have been able to stop them," she said. I clung onto her.

"I'd better go down to the police station to be with them," said Dad. "They'll be glad of my support."

"Yes, please go, Jack. The police must have made a mistake."

My father left and Mum sat me on her knee and gave me a cuddle. He returned with bad news. All three lads had been charged and were due in court the following morning. Sam and Larry were held on remand, but Tim was allowed home on bail. I felt awkward when I went to school next day as it was the latest village gossip.

"It's not your fault, Christine, you're not to blame," said Sheila. "My mother told me to be nice to you." My friends understood, so I stayed close to them in the playground. Some of the children called me names and said nasty things about my brothers. I went home and cried to my mother.

"Just tell them that sticks and stones may break your bones, but words will never hurt you," she told me. I didn't think this was true because their words had already hurt me.

Chapter Eight

WHEN THE COURT case came around, my parents went to support the boys. I had the day off school and Mrs Hendy looked after me. She had just bought a television which my parents hoped would be a distraction.

"What's a television?" I asked.

"We haven't got time to explain, you'll see," they said.

I was engrossed in The Lone Ranger when my parents returned with the news that Sam had been sent to jail for 18 months. Mrs Hendy helped my mother to a chair. "Whoever would have thought it would come to this?" said Mrs Hendy. "Sam has always been such a good boy. I can't believe it."

I started crying because I didn't want Sam sent away. I was worried about him going to prison, though I didn't truly understand what that meant.

"I can't believe it either," sobbed Mum.

"We're very relieved that Tim has been given probation," said Dad.

"Thank goodness for that," said Mrs Hendy, "considering he spent all that time in hospital as a boy."

"Yes, that's what worried us," said Dad. "We know that he's the weakest. Sam will probably go to Exeter prison, but Larry's going to a Borstal, the youth detention centre, because he's too young for prison."

"He was the ringleader though, wasn't he?" Mrs Hendy asked.

"Yes, he was in with a bad crowd before he joined the RAF. He led Sam and Tim astray," Mum replied, tears streaming down her face.

"I love you, Mummy," I said, holding her hand.

"I know you do, Christine," she said, squeezing it. "Well, thank Mrs Hendy for looking after you and letting you watch her television."

I thanked Mrs Hendy, who said I could go there to watch television any time. Over tea my parents wrestled with how this had happened to their sons just as they'd seemed to be doing so well.

"I thought I'd done my best by them," said Dad.

"Now everyone in the village is going to be talking about us," said Mum. "I'm so ashamed."

The latch on the gate went and Tim walked in. "Those bloody magistrates had it in for us," he said. "Pompous sods."

"I did warn Sam," said Dad. "I'd have thought he'd have had more sense."

Tim shot Dad a filthy look. "Didn't expect you to understand, old man," he said.

"Seeing as it was Sam's first offence, you'd think they would have been more lenient," said Mum.

"I believe that they decided to make an example of you all," said Dad. "That's Sam's RAF career finished. I did warn him, but as always, he knew best."

"Trust you, old man. It sounds as if you're on their side."

"Far from it, son, but it beats me how Sam thought he could get away with it. I'm very disappointed that he dragged you into it."

Tim sprang to Sam's defence. "It's not Sam's fault, it was my decision to go along."

"I blame you, Jack," said Mum. "Why in the world didn't you let me know what was going on?"

"You weren't well, Ruby, I didn't want to worry you with it."

"Well it's all a bit late now," she said. "Come on, Tim. Sit down and have your tea."

"I don't feel hungry. Stick it." And with that he picked up his bag and stomped up the stairs.

When I woke next morning the first thing I remembered was that Sam had been sent to prison. I felt sad as it dawned on me I wouldn't be hearing him singing and whistling any more. I was worried about what the other children were going to say. Mum told me to ignore them, but also said I'd be going for lunch each day with Aunty Mary at the Jolly Miller so she could keep an eye on me.

The day went okay at school. Only a few children teased me and most importantly my friends stood by me. A few days later we received a letter from Sam saying Exeter prison wasn't so bad.

Tim was struggling with his probation officer. My brother felt the court official had it in for him. Fortunately, he'd managed to keep his job at the jewellers' shop, but he needed to meet the probation officer each day after work. He couldn't get there in time and was fast getting on the wrong side of him. Tim couldn't leave work early or his pay would be docked.

"I'll have to run from work to meet the officer," he said.

"I know it's hard, Tim," said Mum. "We care about you, don't we, Christine?"

"Yes, we care about you, Tim," I said, hugging him.

Life fell into a routine but something had changed in Tim. He was angry and resentful. He complained about the food on the table. One particular day when Dad told him to be grateful, he kicked off, accusing our father of preferring Sam to him.

"I remember you kicking me when I didn't want to go to church," Tim yelled.

"I didn't treat you any different from Sam."

"I always got the worst of it." Tim was still shouting. "You knew how to put the boot in."

"I feel sorry now," said Dad. "I didn't know that you didn't want to go because there was a gang waiting to throw stones at you. I thought you were making it up just to get out of going to church."

"It was cruel of you," said Tim.

Mum and I stopped eating. She looked very upset and I felt really worried.

"I'm sorry. I thought I was doing the right thing."

"Well you weren't," snarled Tim. "I wouldn't think twice

about slitting your throat, old man."

I looked at Tim in horror as he pulled a razor from his top pocket.

"Don't be silly, son," said Dad.

But Tim knew he had the upper hand. Mother screamed at him, "Don't, Tim, don't!"

"The old man's not so brave now," Tim sneered. "Look, Mother!"

"Stop waving that razor around," she said sharply.

"Who is going to stop me?"

"Behave, Tim. You'll do as you're told while you're living here," said Dad.

"You don't think I'm afraid of you now, do you?"

"For goodness sake, think of your mother. She's been ill and it's not right to behave like this in front of your little sister."

Dad's words didn't seem to register with Tim. I had never felt fear like it.

"You're scared now, old man, don't want any trouble?" Tim gloated, getting closer and closer with the razor.

"That's enough! If you can't behave, pack your bags and leave." At that moment my father saw his opportunity and made a grab for the razor.

"Get lost," screamed Tim, and threw the razor across the room. I was frozen to the spot as the razor hit the wall and ricocheted onto the floor right beside Dad. Mum breathed a sigh of relief as my father managed to retrieve the blade.

"I think I'd better hang on to this," he said. "It's obvious to me you can't be trusted with it."

"To hell with you. If you want me to leave, I'll go," Tim yelled. "I don't know why anyone would want to live in a dump like this anyway, it's a bloody slum."

He ran upstairs to pack his bags and looked even more furious when he came back down.

Mum grabbed his arm. "Please don't go, son. I don't want you to leave," she pleaded, tears running down her face.

"No, I'm going, Mother. I can't live here any longer. I'll let you know when I've found somewhere else to live."

He walked out and slammed the door, leaving a stunned silence.

Dad tried to convince Mum that Tim would come home, but he didn't. A few weeks later he wrote to say he had transferred probation officer and had a new job in a jewellers' in Leicester and had found lodgings. I was glad Tim was okay although I was sad he'd left.

Without her boys, Mum was desperately unhappy. Dad suggested we take a day out in town to try and raise our spirits. Mum wanted to buy a radio and he wanted to change his books at the stall in the market house that operated a bit like a library. You could buy books, and after reading them you could return them, and they would give you money off further books you bought.

Mum wore her favourite red dress. With her hair tied in a bun I thought she was looking better than she'd done for ages. We went to the book stall first and Dad exchanged his books and let me choose some too. I was glad as I'd just begun to read well enough to be able to read my own stories. I picked out two that I liked and stood waiting patiently for Dad. I knew he bought a lot of books to take to work so he could read in between the jobs he had to do in the pump house. Dad soon had a pile of books and I gave him mine to pay for.

We went to the radio shop and Mum picked a red and cream set. We went to a café, where my parents had tea and I had a slice of chocolate cake and a glass of fizzy lemonade. We called into a few more shops along the way before we arrived at Woolworths. Dad thought we could get some cheap batteries for the radio and Mum said I could have some Jelly Babies.

As we walked back to catch the bus, we saw the Paddington-to-Penzance steam train pulling in at the railway station. It was thrilling as the steam from the engine billowed out, forming white clouds above the platform. I watched the guard as he went along slamming the doors shut before blowing his whistle. As the train chuffed out of the station I waved at the passengers looking out of the windows, and to my delight they waved back until all the coaches disappeared out of sight.

Back at home we ate tea before my parents put the battery-powered radio on and listened to a game show programme called Have a Go with Wilfred Pickles, whose catchphrase was, "What's on the table, Mabel?" I got myself comfy on the settee and started reading my book. It was funny and made me chuckle. All in all it had been a good day.

The next morning Dad did some gardening before leaving for work. He packed his crib bag with saffron buns and some cheese, and he was off.

"I'll put on the radio, Christine, and see what's on," said Mum, as she tuned into Radio Luxembourg so we could listen to

DJs playing songs we liked to sing along to. I liked the top 10, as when I went to school I could talk to my friends about it. It made me feel less left out when they were talking about TV programmes, as the only time I managed to watch TV was when I was able to visit Mrs Hendy. Radio Luxembourg became something Mum and I really enjoyed listening to together.

One night she asked me to be quiet as she was keen to hear a man named Horace Batchelor who claimed he could help people win the football pools with his new Infra-Draw Method. "I think I will write his details down, Christine," she picked up a pen and piece of paper. "He is claiming to have won a lot of money on the football pools, I think I will send him my name and address and find out more about it."

"It would be lovely if he could help you win," I said.

My father encouraged her to give it a go. She started giving me letters to post, then one evening I came home from school to find her looking extremely excited.

"I've won the pools!"

"That's wonderful, Mummy!" I said, hoping she would be able to buy a house down Carlyon Bay and that Dad could stop working.

"Yes, fifty pounds. I wouldn't have managed that without the Infra-Draw Method."

Dad arrived home from work. "I've won the pools, Jack!" she called out.

"What? You've really won?"

"Fifty pounds!" she said, waving her winning cheque.

"A nice amount," said Dad, giving her a kiss. "But not enough for me to give up work."

"I'll keep trying, Jack. It just proves it's possible."

I could see she was thrilled to bits at winning, she'd got the bug. I continued posting letters for her and she had several smaller wins, but nothing substantial.

One evening after doing PE I came home from school really hungry. "What can I have for tea?" I asked.

Mum looked worried. "I'm sorry, Christine. The only thing left is a couple of slices of bread and a bit of margarine," she said. "I'll tell you what, why don't you go out in the garden and pick some of Dad's spring onions? You can eat them with bread and margarine."

"Yes, I'll do that," I said, knowing I didn't have any option. I went to the garden and pulled up some spring onions, took them back in and gave them to her. I watched as she washed them, cut them up and sprinkled salt and vinegar on them.

"There you are, Christine, it's the best I can do," she told me. I was glad when Dad brought a few bits of shopping home.

After this I would often arrive home from school to find nothing in the cupboards. During half term, a man called at the door saying he was buying antiques and jewellery. I stood watching as Mum brought some of her best jewellery to the door. I felt dismayed when I saw several pieces that had belonged to her mother. There was a discussion about the price, and after a bit of haggling, she agreed to sell them.

"Why did you sell your favourite necklace, Mummy?" I asked.

"I had to sell it, Christine. We need the money dear," she

said. She gave a sigh. "Please don't be worried, I'll win lots of money soon."

I hoped she was right and felt relieved later that day when the baker's van arrived and she bought a loaf and some jam for my tea.

"I love bread and jam, Mummy," I said.

"I'm glad you enjoyed it, Christine." I noticed she hadn't had any herself, but had made do with a cup of tea and a couple of Rich Tea biscuits. "If I give you some money tomorrow, could you call in the post office and get me a postal order?" she asked.

"Yes of course, Mummy."

"I would love to win in time for your eighth birthday," she said. "I hear a lot of people are getting rich using the Infra-Draw Method."

"I hope so, Mummy. It would be lovely if Daddy could stay at home with you."

"It would make me the happiest woman alive," she said. "Let's put the radio on. When I win the pools, we will get a house with electric and be able to have television too.

Chapter Nine

SAM WAS DUE home after serving his sentence. Dad had gone to work but Mum had kept me home from school so I could welcome him.

"Don't forget to give him a big hug," she reminded me. "He kept telling me in his letters how much he was missing you."

"I will, Mummy."

Sam was later than hoped and Mum became incredibly anxious as she looked out for him. When he finally came through the gate, I ran towards him and he picked me up and squeezed me, carrying me inside. "I'm home, Mother," he called out.

The three of us hugged as tears ran down Mum's face. "Don't cry, Mother," Sam said. "I'm home now. You don't have to worry anymore. I don't intend to end up back inside again, I can tell you that."

"You made a mistake but that's in the past," she said. "Your room's ready and bed made up."

"That's great, but what have you got to eat?" Sam walked

over to the cupboard in the living room where the Cornish range was, opened it and took a step backwards. "Have you got something ready for me in the kitchen?" he asked, making his way there.

"I'm sorry, Sam, your father's getting some groceries when he leaves work," she said. "Christine had the last piece of bread when she had milk sops"

"Why didn't the old man get something in?" Sam demanded. "I've heard all the other guys bragging about going home to a three-course lunch."

Mum looked upset and I began to wish I hadn't eaten the last piece of bread. "I'm sorry, son. Could you go up to the village to get something?" I've got five shillings in my purse."

Sam didn't look impressed. "You mean I've got to go to the shops before I can have something to eat? What's wrong with father? He knew I was coming home?"

Mum lowered her head and shrugged. "You know what it's like, Sam. We've been short of money," she said.

"Do you want me to get something for you and Christine?" he asked.

"Could you get a loaf, two cans of soup and a packet of biscuits?"

Sam looked downcast – it wasn't the homecoming he'd expected. "Is my old bicycle in the shed?" he asked. "It would be better than walking."

"Yes, your bike's still there, Sam."

He went out to the shed and came back looking even more upset. "The bloody tyres are flat and the bicycle pump's missing.

I'll have to walk."

He stormed out the door, my mother calling after him that she was sorry. When Sam returned he was looking a bit happier. "Here, Christine. I managed to get you something to eat," he said. "And guess what else I got you?"

I looked at him as he pulled a packet of sweets from his pocket. "Thanks, Sam," I said, giving him another big hug. "I've missed you loads."

"I've missed you too," he said. "I haven't been able to pull your leg for ages." He smiled and looked a bit more relaxed. I watched as he started to slice up the bread and heat up the soup. Mum looked so relieved.

"I'm sorry, Sam," she said again. "Since I had my stroke it's been harder for me to get to the shops."

"Don't worry, Mother, I'll soon get a job and then I'll be able to help you out."

We chatted as we ate. Sam said he was going to visit Jim Hendy who had written to him while he was in prison. Jim's sister, Violet, was getting married. Sam was surprised to hear this as Jim hadn't mentioned it.

"No doubt because Jim doesn't think anyone's good enough for her!" said Mum. "I can see Violet ending up an old maid if she takes notice of Jimmy."

Sam started laughing. "Not everyone wants to get married."

"Christine does, don't you?" she asked me.

"Yes I do, Mummy, and have a lovely wedding like Victoria."

"Victoria is having another baby," said Mum. "A little brother or sister for Paula"

"So Aunty Alice is going to be a granny again," Sam said.

"She's thrilled to bits. I'm hoping that you'll find a nice young lady and settle down."

Sam raised his eyebrows. "I can't promise that," he said. "Don't rush me."

When Dad came home he apologised to Sam for not having got back with food before he'd arrived. He set about cooking egg, bacon and chips. "We've got to welcome Sam home," he said.

I couldn't wait to go to school to tell Miss Truscott and Sheila that Sam was home the next day. At lunchtime I made my way down to the Jolly Miller with a spring in my step, ready to explode with the news. When I walked in, Aunty Mary had just finished serving a customer and came out from the bar.

"Hello, Christine, we've got Welsh rarebit today," she said.

"Sam's come home!" I said thrilled to be able to tell her.

"I'm so glad, I've always been fond of Sam," said Aunty Mary, sounding relieved.

Sam went out every day to try and find work, but it was a struggle. He tried Little John's clay works and several clay pits, and grew convinced the reason he couldn't get work was because he'd just come out of prison. Dad tried to reassure him that it was just because there wasn't a lot of work about. Eventually Sam decided to make a fresh start and go and live with Tim. My heart sank when he told us.

"Give it a bit more time, Sam," said Mum.

"No, I've made up my mind. I can't keep scrounging off you. Tim's found somewhere for me to stay and I'm going up to Leicester with him next week."

I felt really sad and could see from Mum's face that she did too. She said she would wash all his clothes ready and that we would have a wonderful weekend together. Sam was extra nice to me.

"Make sure you're a good girl, Christine," he said. "We'll both come down at Christmas and bring you a present."

"How long is it before Christmas?" I asked.

"Not long, just a few months. I know that you'll be looking forward to it"

"I will," I said. "I haven't seen Tim for ages."

"We'll come down and have a lovely family Christmas together, playing games and roasting nuts by the fire."

Sam's promise cheered me up, and when I waved him off I busied my mind with thoughts of Christmas. It wasn't long before my mother received a letter from Sam letting her know that he had found a job with an engineering firm. He wrote later to say that he and Tim wouldn't make it down for Christmas. Tim had to work late on Christmas Eve and there was no train that could get them home in time. Sam didn't want to leave Tim to have Christmas on his own. My heart sank and I was bitterly disappointed about it.

"They are going to post your Christmas presents down for you, Christine," Mum told me as she finished reading the letter. "I expect they'll come down at Easter."

I felt tears sting my eyes.

"Well, we'll still have a lovely Christmas, the three of us," said Dad trying to cheer me up. But I knew it wouldn't be the same without my brothers.

* * *

I didn't quite believe it when my friends at school told me there was no such thing as Father Christmas. I was as excited as ever, tearing open paper from carefully wrapped gifts. Mum and Dad heard me shout and came into my room to see me.

Mum pointed to an especially large one. "This one's from Sam and Tim."

I ripped open the box from Sam and Tim and squealed with delight. "Look!" Tim has sent me a massive paint box with loads of different coloured paints! And Sam's put in lot of colouring books!"

My parents were over the moon with my reaction. I opened another present and found it was a beautiful soft, pink fluffy jumper.

"That one is from Aunty Alice," said Mum. "She'll change it for you if it doesn't fit."

I tried it on right away and looked in the mirror.

"It fits you just right," said Mum. "Do you like it?"

"Yes it's lovely and soft," I told her.

I opened another present and let out a cry. "See what Aunty Mary's got me!" It was a fantastic pink net underskirt with satin ribbons. "I love it, all the girls are wearing them, it's the latest fashion," I said, over the moon to have one.

"It's lovely to look at, Christine, but not as practical as the warm jumper from Aunty Alice," said Mum.

"Yes, the jumper will be what you need most during the winter," said Dad.

I looked around the room and couldn't see anything from my parents. They laughed at my expression. "If you want to see what you got from us you'll have to go downstairs," said Dad.

I could feel the suspense building as I ran downstairs. As soon as I entered the room I saw a large object wrapped in brown paper.

"What is it?" I asked full of excitement and anticipation.

"You'll have to open it to find out," Dad told me.

As the paper ripped away, I saw the shiny chrome handlebars. I couldn't contain my excitement and pulled off the wrapping as fast as I could. I gasped when I saw a gleaming, magnificent maroon-red bicycle. I ran over to my parents and threw my arms around them.

"We thought it was about time you had a bike," said Dad. "Once you learn to ride you can ride to school and not rely on a lift from Miss Truscott."

I couldn't take my eyes off my bike; it was such a beautiful colour, with shiny stainless-steel mudguards.

"It's the best Christmas present I've ever had," I gasped. "Can I go out and ride it?"

"Yes of course, love, after we've had Christmas dinner I'll come out with you," said Dad.

My parents were thrilled to see how much I loved my bike. We all went back upstairs to get dressed and my parents put the dinner in the oven.

My paints and colouring books kept me busy as I waited for dinner. The smell of chicken roasting filled the air and I began to feel hungry. "Put those painting books away now, Christine," said

Dad, "dinner's nearly ready. Only the three of us so there is plenty to go around. We'll even be able to have chicken sandwiches later on."

The food was wonderful but we all wished Sam and Tim were there to share it with us. After lunch Dad exchanged his slippers for his boots. "Let's go out, Christine, and you can practise riding your bike," he said.

He lifted the bike down the steps into the back yard. "You can have a practise on the garden path and I'll hold the back of your bike steady."

Mum came out to watch, smiling as I wobbled from side to side, struggling to get my balance. "I had the same problem when I was learning to ride a bike, Christine," she said. "Once you get the hang of it, there'll be no stopping you."

I was so excited, as once I could ride I knew I'd be able to go and visit my friends and help Mum with errands such as collecting milk from the farm.

I was doing well when it started to rain. "We better go back inside," said Dad. "We don't want to get wet"

"Yes, come on in now. I'll put the kettle on for a cuppa and we can have some Christmas cake," said Mum.

I couldn't resist so we put my bike in the wash house and went inside. But whenever I could, I continued to ride, and soon Dad said I was good enough to go on the road and then all the way to school. My parents decided to buy Miss Truscott a gift to thank her for all the lifts. Mum had been doing well, winning small amounts on the football pools so we decided to go shopping in town. I chose a scarf for Miss Truscott and Mum said she would pick her flowers from the garden.

Chapter Ten

ON THE FINAL day of spring term, when Miss Truscott came to collect me, my mother explained I'd be riding my bike to school after the Easter holidays. Miss Truscott was very happy for me and delighted with her scarf and lovely flowers. I was looking forward to being independent and told Mum during the holidays I'd ride up to Farmer Foster's to collect her milk.

The last day of school was fun. We sang a rousing rendition of All Things Bright and Beautiful in assembly, then back in class Miss Truscott got the paints out to whoops of delight from all of us. She wanted us to paint our homes, so I painted Fir Tree Cottage complete with porch and the fir tree near the gate where my swing hung between the branches.

As I painted, I chatted with my friends about something the headmaster had announced during assembly. He'd told us that there would be exams in the summer term and that we shouldn't worry as there would be extra classes for anyone who was behind. I was nine, and relieved to hear that, because my mother's illness had caused me to fall behind.

All that was forgotten when I went to Aunty Mary's for lunch. I wanted to pet her dog, Bosun, and found him in the back yard curled up with the pig. I couldn't stop laughing as I scratched his head – Bosun, not the pig, who just grunted.

Aunty Mary came to find me. "I've got you a nice Cornish pasty, one I made this morning," she said.

"I love your pasties, Aunty Mary," I said, munching away as Bosun looked on enviously. When I'd finished, Aunty Mary opened up the cake tin. I chose a very tempting looking bun with a cherry on top.

"Who else can I spoil if I can't spoil my niece?" said Aunty Mary. "I'll just get you some lemonade with it being the last day of term and all that."

Aunty Mary brought me a long glass full of delicious lemonade with loads of bubbles, which I tried to stop from going up my nose.

Back at school, Sheila was playing with a hula hoop she'd been given for Christmas. I'd never seen one before so was delighted when she invited me to have a go. On the first few tries, the hoop kept falling to the ground. Sheila tried to teach me how to do it. Maureen couldn't get the hang of it either.

"It takes a bit of practise," said Sheila.

"Where did you get it?" I asked.

"Woolworths," she replied. "They've got them in lots of different colours."

Sheila's was blue but I decided I wanted a red one. Maureen was worried that her mother wouldn't be able to afford hula hoops for her and her sister, so I said that if I got one she could share it, which cheered her up. Back in class we tidied our desks then played Happy Families and Snap. We had a lovely time that afternoon and I felt sorry when it was time to go home. I walked down with Miss Truscott and got in her car. It seemed strange to think that when I came back to school I wouldn't be riding with her any more.

Miss Truscott opened the door for me. "Are your brothers coming home for Easter, Christine?" she asked.

"No, Miss, they're hoping to come down in the summer though," I said. I'd been disappointed when I heard this news from Mum.

When Miss Truscott dropped me off both my parents were home. Dad asked me if Miss Truscott was happy with her gift and I told him about Sheila's hula hoop. "Can I get one please, Daddy?" I asked.

"Well, it all depends on how much they cost," he said. "Where can you buy them?"

"Woolworths. Can I get one when we go in town?"

"We'll see."

Mum piped up then. "I'll buy her one with the money I've won. I'll get Aunty Alice to get it," she said. I was so happy; I gave her a kiss.

"You're lucky, Christine," said Dad.

"And you'll think yourself even luckier when you see the size of the Easter egg that Sam and Tim have sent you," said Mum, producing an enormous parcel.

My chin must have dropped in disbelief because neither of

my parents could stop laughing at my expression. The egg was huge and full of sweets.

"Just a little each day," said Mum, "or you'll make yourself ill. I'll put it in my wardrobe until Easter Sunday."

Dad and I went into the garden to pick peas and dig potatoes for tea. He'd bought some ham on the way home from work and we enjoyed a tasty tea, with Mum making sweet comments about how well Dad looked after us. We washed and dried up together before I went outside to play with my ball, which I loved bouncing against the wall.

The next morning, as promised, I cycled to Farmer Foster's for milk. Mum gave me a canvas bag that fitted on top of my bicycle's mudguard. "Are you sure you know the way?" she asked.

"Of course," I said. "I've been there loads of times."

"Be careful then."

"I will, Dad told me to pull in if I see a lorry."

She handed me the money and off I went, feeling very grown up and proud. Mrs Foster admired my bike when I arrived at the farm. I noticed a pretty little girl with blonde hair standing beside the milk shed door. I gave her a smile.

"You haven't met Christine have you, Lucy?" Mrs Foster asked her.

Lucy looked shy but wandered over. "Hello, I like your bike."

"It was a Christmas present." I told her.

"Go and get your bike, Lucy, and show Christine," said Mrs Foster. Lucy ran off and returned with her bike.

"Your bike is nice as well," I said. "I like blue."

"You two should make friends," said Mrs Foster. "You could go riding together."

My heart leapt for joy at the thought. "I'd love to be friends," I said.

"You could ride in and out of the lane. Lucy still needs practise," Mrs Foster added.

"I could help her," I said.

"Ask your mother if you can come round tomorrow," said Mrs Foster.

"I hope she lets you," Lucy said.

"Yes, I'm sure she will. What time?"

"Around ten would be fine," said Mrs Foster. "We've finished milking by that time of the morning."

The mention of milking reminded me I needed two pints. Lucy helped me put the milk into the canvas bag and I got on my bike ready to cycle home.

"See you tomorrow," Lucy called out as I cycled away. I was so excited to have a new friend. Back at Fir Tree Cottage, I rushed inside. "I've just met Lucy, Mrs Foster's granddaughter, and she wants to be my friend," I gasped.

"What? Did you see Lucy today?"

"Yes, and she's got a bike like mine, Mummy. But hers is blue."

"It'd be nice for you to be friends," she said. "But be kind to Lucy."

"I'm always kind, Mummy," I said.

"I know you are, Christine. But it's a difficult time for Lucy. She lost her mother recently."

"Why? What's happened to her?"

"Her mother passed away, that's why she's come to live near her granny."

I was heartbroken at hearing this. "Well, I'll be extra kind then," I said.

"And don't mention it to Lucy. Talking about it might make her cry."

"I know," I said. "Just like when you were ill, Mummy, and I was upset."

I went over and hugged her. "I love you," I said, feeling grateful she hadn't died.

"You're such a sensitive little soul, Christine," she said. "You'll make a good friend for Lucy."

When Dad came home I told him about going to get the milk and about making friends with Lucy. He was really happy for me.

* * *

I opened my eyes the following morning and immediately remembered Lucy. I ate a bowl of cornflakes, washed and dressed, and was raring to go. Mum gave me money for two pints of milk and told me to be home by 5pm.

When I arrived at the farm I knew the milking had been done when I saw several churns ready for collection. Lucy was waiting for me and ran over to open the gate.

Lucy suggested we go and see her Aunty Pat. I'd heard my parents talking about her the night before as she was now looking after Lucy and her little brother, Liam, who was three. I was anxious about meeting Aunty Pat and hoped she would like me, but I needn't have worried. She was a lovely woman, very warm and welcoming. Lucy and I stayed there for a while, drinking orange juice and playing with Liam, who I thought was cute.

After a while we went off on our bikes. Lucy knew the area well and I was glad she was with me, especially when a dog barked at us from one of the farms we passed. Lucy reassured me that he was friendly.

"There's another cottage at the end of the lane. I have cousins living there, but they're a lot older." Lucy told me.

"You are lucky," I said. "My two brothers are away and I miss them."

"Well, you've got me for company now," she said. "Whenever you're bored, or want something to do, come up to see me."

We reached the end of the lane and went through a gate onto moorland, where we decided to make a den amid the ferns. I found some that were quite dense and we trampled them down so the middle was hollow and the ferns on the outside higher. We were well concealed, and it was a good place to hide. We chatted away. I told her about my family and was disappointed to learn that Lucy wouldn't be going to the same school as me.

"Don't worry," said Lucy. "We can still see each other at the weekends and in the holidays."

After a while we were hungry so decided to head back to Aunty Pat's. "Don't forget to keep our little den a secret," said Lucy as we crept out through a gap in the ferns and rearranged them so that no one would know.

"I won't tell anyone," I agreed. I loved having a secret place to share with Lucy. I'd read about secret dens in some of my books.

Over lunch, Aunty Pat made me feel really at home. Afterwards we rode up and down the lane until Lucy suggested we walk across the field so that we could feed the Fosters' chickens. The field was full of daisies, so we made daisy chains. Lucy had never done that before so I showed her how to make a necklace. She loved doing it and made one for Liam too. Aunty Pat called for us. It was time for me to go home. Lucy took me to get my milk and we arranged to meet the next day.

Lucy had given me some of her Easter egg, so the next day I took mine up to share with her, waiting until we arrived at the den to have a nice feast there. I spent as much time as possible with Lucy that Easter, going to our den most days. But all too soon the holiday was over. I would miss Lucy but I was excited to show my school friends how much I'd improved with my bike riding.

The day before school, I cleaned my bike before dinner. Afterwards, Dad put the kettle on and collected the bath from the washhouse, where there was a coal-fuelled boiler for washing clothes. I watched as he lifted the bath down from a nail on the wall. Mum filled it from the kettle that had boiled on the Cornish range, and I was soon splashing in the water in the living room.

"How are you doing?" she asked. "Have you washed behind your ears?"

"Yes, and I've scrubbed my feet and in between my toes."

I lifted my feet out of the water as she came over to look.

"They're all right but pass me the soap and flannel and I'll wash your back."

She washed my hair, helped me out of the bath and wrapped me in a towel. I dried myself as she went to get my nightdress, before tucking me into bed. "Goodnight, sleep tight," she said, kissing me on the forehead. I fell asleep thinking how it had been the best holiday ever.

The next morning I called for Sheila on my way to school. She told me about her holidays and going to the cinema, and I told her about playing with Lucy. She waited for me as I dropped my bike off at the Jolly Miller.

It was great to be back at school. I went to see Aunty Mary at lunch time and told her about Lucy and the enormous Easter egg Sam and Tim had sent.

"Ah, that's lovely Christine," she said. "You are a lucky girl. And guess what? I've got another surprise for you. It's what Aunty Alice said you wanted."

"What is it?" I asked.

"A hula hoop," she replied.

I couldn't believe my luck. I had given up hope of getting one. I was so happy when Aunty Mary came back carrying a bright red hula hoop. "Oh, thank you, Aunty Mary!" I said. "Thank you so much."

"You can take it to school if you like," she said. "Leave it in the outhouse when you come to collect your bike."

I ran back to school as quickly as I could and let Maureen have the first go. The weeks flew by as I rode my bike to school, went out with Lucy at the weekends, and hula hooped and

AN INNOCENT GIRL

skipped with my chums.

Chapter Eleven

MUM RECEIVED A letter from Sam and Tim. They had moved to London where Sam had found a higher paid job. Tim found work in a jewellers' shop and they'd managed to find bedsits in North London.

"When are they coming down to see us?" I asked.

"I don't expect they have the time with them working so many hours," said Dad as he read Tim's latest letter. "Tim's working all week in the jewellers' shop and has a stall down Petticoat Lane at weekends."

"Where's Petticoat Lane, Dad?"

"It's where traders set up stalls and sell things," he replied. "Look, Tim's put something in for you." He handed me a packet and I ripped it open in excitement. Something dropped out and jumped across the table.

"It's a jumping bean," said Mum.

I looked in the packet and found more. I was thrilled and decided to take them to school to show my friends. They all asked me where they came from and I was proud to say Petticoat Lane; it sounded so exciting.

After this I often received gifts from Petticoat Lane. Such as a drinking duck and a music box, which kept me amused for hours. But there was no visit from my brothers. I got used to it and enjoyed having fun with my school friends and seeing Lucy at weekends.

The summer holidays were coming and Lucy and I were planning some nice Aunty-Pat picnics by a stream. Lucy suggested we take swimming costumes and have a paddle. My costume no longer fitted so Mum ordered me one from her catalogue, and some sandals too. Lucy's father had promised to take us to the beach. It was a great start to the holidays and I felt elated and as excited as could be.

That first day with Lucy, Aunty Pat had gone all out. We had hard-boiled egg sandwiches, cheese scones, fondant fancies and lemonade. When we got to the stream I remembered Tim taking me there to collect tadpoles. "I'd take them to school so we could watch them turn into frogs," I told Lucy.

We started eating our picnic quite early. I told her how much I loved the fondant fancies and she said Aunty Pat bought them every week.

"I wish I lived with you then," I joked.

I relished every bite and listened as Lucy told me that Aunty Pat had suggested we enter the village carnival dressed as two naughty school girls.

"I've never been in a carnival," I told her. "Tell Aunty Pat I'd love to."

We spent a happy day paddling and chatting. I felt as if I'd never had so much fun. Towards the end of the day, Lucy asked if I wanted to go to Sunday school with her.

"It will give you chance to meet other children who'll be in the carnival too," she said. I was keen and said I'd speak to Mum about it. Back at Foster's Farm I collected the milk, and as I sailed down the hill towards home, I felt a warm breeze ruffle my hair, giving me a sense of freedom which I'd never felt before.

Back at home, Mum agreed we should enter the carnival. Having eaten the picnic early I was feeling hungry and opened the cupboard. It was empty.

"Dad hasn't been shopping yet," said Mum. She sounded a bit worried.

I didn't want to worry her so I told her all about the picnic and how I wasn't that hungry anyway. She suggested I go outside and pick some strawberries. I did that and dug up some carrots too. I handed the strawberries to Mum for her to eat and she peeled the carrots for me.

The next day Dad was going to Foster's Farm to help bring in the hay. He asked if I wanted to go and I felt keen to see what it was all about. I knew Lucy would be there too.

When we arrived in the field we saw a lot of the hay had already been cut. We had to collect it and stack it in square bales, which my father knew how to do. This was so it was ready for storing in the hayloft. As we were gathering the hay, I scared a tiny field mouse and watched it race away. Farmer Foster appeared with his tractor and trailer and drove into the field. Men, including Dad, loaded the bales on the trailer, and Farmer

Foster drove the load to the barn. When he returned, he asked Dad if he could help with bringing in the corn later in the week. Dad said he had some days off and would be glad to help.

At lunchtime, Lucy's granny brought out her home-cured ham sandwiches and some lemonade.

"If you think this is good, wait until the end of the week," said Lucy.

"Why, what happens at the end of the week?"

"When the harvest has been brought in, Granny brings out a spread so we can celebrate. It's amazing."

After lunch we worked for a few more hours then went home to rest our aching backs. The farmer had given Dad some money and I could see that he was pleased to hand it over to Mum.

"You've caught the sun," Mum told me. "You're as brown as a berry! You're a real country girl and you look healthy as can be."

The next day the ache in my back had gone and I jumped out of bed ready to go up to see Lucy and get my carnival outfit sorted. Aunty Pat was well prepared and had everything ready for me. I could see that Lucy looked the part with a tennis racket in her hand. Aunty Pat gave me a toy gun to carry as she couldn't find anything else.

"You both look the part," she said. "You're a pair of cheeky rascals."

The next day we brought in the corn and I discovered that Lucy wasn't kidding about her grandmother's celebratory feast.

"Granny wants us to save some corn so she can make corn dollies," Lucy told me.

"How does she do that?" I asked.

"I don't know but she'll show us if you want. They'll be sold at the carnival with the money going to charity."

* * *

"Christine, your swimming costume and sandals have arrived. Come down and try them on."

I dashed downstairs, still half asleep but keen to take a look. I fell in love with the costume right away; it was such a wonderful turquoise colour.

"Thanks, Mum, it looks lovely," I gasped, looking in the mirror.

"You look neat and tidy now for going to the beach," she replied.

I went off to see Lucy and told her my new costume had arrived. We visited Mrs Hendy, who was moving away. Her children wanted to move so they wouldn't have such a long way to travel to work. I told her about our beach plans and she promised to find us a beach ball she had going spare.

Back at Lucy's, we played with Liam then took him for a walk. My parents had agreed that I could stay later to watch television, so Aunty Pat gave us a lovely tea, followed by strawberry jelly topped with a dab of clotted cream. Then it was time for TV. Liam was excited as he loved to watch Flower Pot Men about Bill and Ben, two little men made of flower pots who lived in a garden. I had never seen it before. When I got home, Mum gave me the beach ball Mrs Hendy had brought over.

Mum was sad that our lovely neighbour was moving away.

Dad wondered who we might get as neighbours and I hoped they'd have children. Once I was in bed, I felt sad about Mrs Hendy moving. It was only thinking about going to the beach with Lucy that stopped me from crying.

The next day was Sunday and Mum insisted I wore my best dress – a pink and white candy stripe, which everyone said looked nice – to Sunday school with Lucy.

I enjoyed singing hymns and loved listening to the Bible stories. Lucy introduced me to some of the other children. We started talking about the carnival and I found out what the other children were doing. When some of the boys decided to go over to the playing field to kick a ball around, Lucy said it was time for us to go home. She asked if I would like to go to Sunday school again, and I said I would. Back at hers, her father Martin reminded me that we were off to the beach that week and to bring a bucket and spade.

"I'll bring my beach ball too," I said.

"And I'll make a nice picnic," said Aunty Pat.

I was so excited when the day finally came for the beach trip. Even the journey was a lot of fun because Lucy started singing and we all joined in. It wasn't long before we were parking up and walking down to the beach. Lucy and I had our swimming costumes on under our clothes so only had to take our dresses off to be ready to play. Lucy spotted a little pool not far from where we were sitting. We went over to do a bit of paddling first. When we looked over, Liam was struggling to build a sandcastle. "Let's go and give him a hand," I said.

Liam got excited as the sandcastle got bigger, until he

knocked it over with his spade. "Never mind," said Lucy. "Let's make another one."

Martin decided he was going for a swim so Lucy and I walked down the beach with him. We both loved the feeling of the waves lapping at our feet. "Stay at the water's edge," Martin told us as he walked out to take the plunge. After splashing about for a while we went back with Aunty Pat and Liam. It wasn't long before Martin started walking back up the beach. He waved to us and we waved back.

"Gosh, I forgot how good it was to swim in the sea," he said.

"Are you ready for the picnic?" asked Aunty Pat.

"Yes, I'm starving, I could eat a horse."

Lucy laughed. "You'd have a job, Dad," she told him. We both started giggling at the thought and Martin was pleased to have amused us.

My tummy was rumbling so I was glad when the picnic came out. Aunty Pat handed me a ham sandwich, which made me think of the ones my mother made when we went to the beach with Sam and Tim.

"Would you like a fondant fancy?" she asked. "Lucy told me how much you liked them. What colour would you like?"

I chose pink before Martin passed me a bottle of ready-mixed orange squash. It looked like a small milk bottle with a silver foil top. I watched Lucy take the top off her bottle, so I did the same.

"Let's go and play with your beach ball, Christine," she said.

Martin blew it up before we headed off down the beach. I felt happy when we bumped into a group of children Lucy knew. We stopped to speak to them and they decided to join in. I was enjoying myself as we threw the ball to one another. There was a lot of screaming and shouting and it felt like the best time ever. All too soon Martin appeared and told us it was time to go home. Lucy and I said goodbye to the other children and went back to help carry everything to the car.

"Thanks for bringing me," I told Martin as he opened the car door.

"It's been a pleasure," he said. "I'm glad Lucy has you for a friend."

The following day when I went up to Lucy's we talked about nothing but the carnival. It started raining in the afternoon so Lucy pulled out her dressing-up box and we started trying on different outfits. Liam thought it was funny and wanted to join in. The next day we went to see Lucy's granny and she showed us how to make corn dollies using the last stems of harvested corn and raffia.

"The fair's coming to the village during carnival week," Lucy told me. "Will you go on the swing boats with me?"

"Yes, I'd love to," I said. I told Mum about it as soon as I got home and she opened her purse so she could find me some change.

"You'll need some money," she told me. "We can't expect Aunty Pat to pay for you." I gave her a hug and thanked her.

Chapter Twelve

THE SUN WAS shining on carnival day. Mum gave me milk sops for breakfast. "You don't want to feel hungry on a special day like today," she said.

I ate it as fast as I could because I was keen to get going.

"Ask Aunty Pat to take a photo of you," Mum told me. She'd have loved to come to the carnival but wasn't well enough. She wasn't able to walk very well and couldn't manage in a crowd, and Dad didn't want to go and leave her.

I raced off, arriving at Lucy's in record time to find her already wearing her carnival outfit and eager for me to put mine on. Aunty Pat couldn't stop laughing when she saw us both dressed up.

As we entered the village, a Wurlitzer could be heard and the fairground was pitched in the playing field. The village was crowded with people who had come from far and wide. There was a lot of excitement and a feeling of expectation filled the air. We found ourselves pushing our way through as so many people lined the street.

"Doesn't the Carnival Queen look lovely," I gasped, grabbing Lucy's arm.

She looked beautiful, as did the Fairy Queens sitting beside her in a float adorned with flowers.

We took our places in the procession of floats. Some were decorated with streamers, others with loads of different coloured balloons. I noticed one float had the brass band aboard, playing music as they drove along. Another float I couldn't take my eyes off ferried nursery-rhyme characters.

It wasn't long before the procession was ready to leave and we made our way through the streets. I'd never seen so many people shouting, waving and cheering. Lucy and I got quite a bit of attention as we passed by and we gave a special wave to Aunty Pat, who was holding Liam and grinning from ear to ear. Suddenly a man walking on stilts joined the procession. It was fascinating to see him taking such big strides. The atmosphere was magical.

As soon as we had completed the planned route, the procession headed back to the playing field. Lucy told me we had to line up so the judges could select the winners. I wasn't sure we would win a prize at all after seeing all the other entries, but we came third in our category and received a book token each.

"What book do you want, Christine?" asked Lucy.

"A Famous Five," I said without hesitating.

"Give me your envelopes, you don't want to lose them," said Aunty Pat. "Let's go to the fair."

Lucy wanted to go on her beloved swing boats first. It was a new experience for me and absolutely thrilling. "Let's see how high we can go," she said, as we both pulled the rope to get started.

After a few more rides and some saffron buns, it was time to go home. I was excited to tell Mum and Dad all about it and show them my book token.

The next day I introduced Lucy to Aunty Alice, who was visiting us at Fir Tree. "So you're Christine's new best friend," Aunty Alice said, smiling at Lucy. "I hear that you've been having a great time during the holidays."

Lucy nodded. "We entered the carnival together."

"We won a prize!" I shouted.

"Well done!" said Aunty Alice.

"It's a book token so would you be able to get me a book?" I asked.

"Yes, which one do you want?"

"Five go to Mystery Moor," I said. "I've wanted it for ages."

"Leave it to me," she said.

Mum and Aunty Alice spoke about my new school uniform, though school was the last thing on my mind. But Mum was right – my old uniform was too small. Aunty Alice measured me and Mum gave her the money to buy one for me.

The rest of the holiday went too quickly. Lucy's father strapped tin cans together to make us stilts and we had a fabulous time walking around on them. Lucy and I agreed it had been a fabulous summer and vowed to meet up every weekend once we were back at school.

I had a new teacher called Mr Sinclair. It seemed strange as we hadn't been taught by a man before, but he was nice and really entertaining. After we had finished our lessons he would start telling us stories about when he was serving in the Navy. He managed to get the boys in the class sitting on the edge of their seats with tales of his ship almost being torpedoed. Most of the girls weren't very impressed but it was more fun than doing lessons.

I continued going to Aunty Mary's for lunch because I had missed her over the holidays. I soon found out that Aunty Mary had a new man friend called Roy who used to come in at lunch time and sit at the table with us. I felt shy of him but he was always nice and pleasant. When Mum heard about it she wasn't very happy.

"You must remember it's been hard for Mary on her own," Dad told her. "She needs someone to help her run The Jolly Miller.

"You have to let people move on, Ruby," agreed Aunty Alice. "It's not easy being a widow."

"I suppose so," said Mum.

The school term moved along and before long we were celebrating harvest festival. I took things Dad had grown in the garden and felt very proud. I loved the thought the food would be going to people in the village who needed it.

* * *

A new couple moved into Mrs Hendy's bungalow. They bought and sold cars and kept themselves to themselves. I saw Lucy at weekends and we both continued attending Sunday school together.

Christmas came and went with a quiet celebration. Dad helped me decorate the tree and put up the decorations. Sam and Tim sent me a present. Again I felt sad they weren't coming home for Christmas; it seemed a very long time since I last saw them both.

I was invited to Lucy's Christmas party and felt pleased to meet her cousins. We played Pass the Parcel, Postman's Knock and several party games. Aunty Pat made lots of treats for us and some very nice jellies.

January was a cold month, with icicles hanging from the window sills in the mornings. I had to walk to school on several occasions because the roads were too icy for me to ride my bike.

The fields were white with frost and when I looked out of the window the grass seemed to sparkle. It was on such a bitter cold day my world fell apart.

"Your mother's had another stroke, Christine," Dad told me when I came home from school. "I'm going to have to take time off work and I've arranged for you to go and stay with Aunty Alice for a while."

I was devastated. Mum was upstairs in bed, and I felt something was wrong as soon as I walked in and she wasn't waiting to welcome me. My mouth dropped open. My dear, lovely little mother was ill again after we all thought she was getting better.

I began to sob. "I want to stay here with Mum," I said.

"Your mother's not able to look after you, love," said Dad. "I'm going to find it hard enough as it is. Be a good girl and go stay with Aunty Alice."

I could see Dad was upset. "I'll phone your brothers tomorrow and see if they'll come home to help out," he said.

"Can't I stay home to look after her?"

"No, you're too young, love. I'll try to get hold of Mrs Lane."

I knew Mrs Lane had helped out before, and I nodded.

"Well you'd better go up and pack your clothes," Dad told me. "Aunty Alice will take you home with her tomorrow."

I had to see Mum before I could even think about packing. "I love you, Mum," I said, leaning over her bed to kiss her forehead. There was no response, she didn't seem to recognise me or even know I was there.

I went into my bedroom to pack before Dad called me downstairs. He'd made some tea but neither of us could eat. I went up to bed and cried myself to sleep. I'd never stayed with Aunty Alice before and didn't know what it would be like. I felt a bit apprehensive because I knew Uncle Will could be quite strict. I hated the idea of leaving my mother.

Aunty Alice arrived the next day looking very worried. "Do you think she's going to be all right, Jack?" she whispered.

"I'm not sure, Alice. It's much worse than before." My father spoke quietly but I still heard.

"Well don't you go worrying about Christine, I'll look after her."

I followed Aunty Alice up the stairs to see Mum before we had to leave. It was heartbreaking seeing her look so unwell. She was as white as a sheet. Aunty Alice spoke to her gently, but she wasn't able to reply. I bent over to kiss her, but again she didn't respond. Tears welled in my eyes as Aunty Alice took my hand and led me downstairs. "Come on, Christine," she said. "We must let your mother rest."

I didn't want to leave my dear mother like this. I kissed Dad goodbye and left Fir Tree Cottage with Aunty Alice, my heart filled with sorrow.

Chapter Thirteen

AN ICY BREEZE penetrated my gloves as I got off the bus. "Let me carry your bag," said Aunty Alice. "We'll soon be home and we can warm up by the fire."

We made our way down the winding hill towards the hamlet, where I caught a glimpse of smoke curling from a chimney. It looked very welcoming and spurred me on against the biting of wind. Eventually we arrived at Hazeldene. Aunty Alice opened the door and I saw Uncle Will in the living room sitting by the fire.

"Come in and warm yourselves" he said, pushing a chair closer to the fire. "Sit here, Christine. I've been keeping my eye on a lovely hotpot for you both."

I sat down and took my gloves off. My fingertips were white. I held my hands in front of the fire and Aunty Alice did the same while Uncle Will took my bag.

"I've put you in Victoria's old bedroom," said Aunty Alice. "I'm sure you'll be comfortable in there."

"Thanks, Aunty Alice," I said.

Uncle Will returned and put the electric light on. I thought how different it was compared to the light of our oil lamp.

We ate our hotpot and Aunty Alice asked if she could tempt me with some trifle. "Yes please," I said.

"No need to ask Uncle Will. He never says no to trifle," she added.

"I can't help it if my wife's a good cook," he said, grinning at me.

"Oh, you're full of flattery," said Aunty Alice.

"I love your cooking, Aunty Alice," I said.

"You're a good girl," she told me.

After we'd eaten, Uncle Will took the dishes to the kitchen and Aunty Alice encouraged me to sit by the fire again. "Let's listen to the radio," she said. "We'll have a rest before doing the dishes."

This routine was new to me so I sat quietly while Aunty Alice and Uncle Will listened to the news and exchanged comments until she headed for the kitchen. "Where do you keep the tea towels, Aunty Alice?" I asked, following her.

"It's bound to be a bit strange for you at first," she said, as she washed and I dried the dishes.

I nodded. When we'd finished it was time to feed the cat, Thomas, and I was told this was to be my job. I was delighted and amazed at the sound he made when I gave him his plate. "I've never heard a cat purr so loudly," I said.

"He's a lovely boy," said Aunty Alice, bending over to smooth him. "Now, we'd better put your clothes away in the wardrobe."

Aunty Alice told me to be sure I kept my room tidy and explained that Uncle Will was very strict about that. I made a mental note of this; I didn't want to upset him.

"Here is your nightdress and some toiletries," she said. I hadn't brought any toiletries and was glad to have them.

I loved the bathroom. It was pure luxury to have warm water on tap, something I had never been used to. Aunty Alice hurried me along from outside the door. "Don't stay in the bathroom too long. Uncle Will won't like it,"

I must have looked surprised when I emerged, because she explained why.

"We don't want a big electricity bill. It costs money to heat the water."

"I'll take care," I said.

"I know you don't have electric at home and wouldn't know about it," she said, putting her arm around my shoulder and guiding me into the bedroom. "I've put a nice hot water bottle in your bed. Have a good sleep. I'll give you a shout in the morning."

She kissed me and left. Although the bed was very comfortable I couldn't sleep for wishing I was at home. I wondered how Mum was and how Dad was coping, shedding a tear or two before finally drifting off.

It instantly dawned on me I wasn't at home when I woke the next morning. There was music playing, which was very soothing.

"You're awake then," said Aunty Alice as she opened the

door. "You'd better get up. You don't want to be late for school."

"Am I going to school today?" I would have liked a day off to come to terms with things.

"I think it would be best, you can walk to school with Sarah."

Sarah was a year younger than me so I didn't know her very well. I felt a bit anxious, but glad at the thought of having someone to walk to school with.

I saw at breakfast that things were much more organised than I was used to. The electric toaster was plugged in and the electric kettle was boiling. I ate cornflakes and toast and drank a cup of tea before I got ready for school and called for Sarah. Her brother, David, was walking with us and did his best to make us laugh. I told Sarah I had two brothers too.

At break time Maureen asked why I'd walked to school with Sarah, and I told her about my mother's stroke. "Oh, I hope she gets better soon," she said.

I hoped the same and found it hard to concentrate on my lessons. I was glad when it was lunchtime and I could go to the pub to see Aunty Mary, and glad, too, that the bar was empty as I could spend more time with her. She was very comforting. "I'm sure your mother will get better," she told me. "She needs a lot of rest and your Dad has done the right thing sending you up to stay with Aunty Alice."

I agreed. "All I want is for Mum to get better," I said.

Aunty Mary gave me a hug. "Everything will be all right, don't you worry."

I enjoyed my pie and mash, followed by ice cream and lemonade, and making a fuss of Bosun. Aunty Mary apologised for him being a bit boisterous, but I never minded.

The afternoon passed quickly enough. Mr Sinclair taught us about Vikings and threw a piece of chalk at Jefferies for talking – he was an excellent shot and hit him on the ear. I walked back with Sarah, and as soon as I was through the door I could tell Aunty Alice had been baking pasties.

"I thought you would like a pasty for tea," she said. "I've made some for your father as well and will take them down tomorrow."

"Can I come with you?"

"It's best you don't at the moment. You go to school and I'll be able to tell you how your mother is in the evening."

I sighed.

"I'll take you down in a week or two," she assured me.

"I miss my mum," I said.

She gave me a hug. "You're bound to, love. Your Dad's still waiting to hear if your brothers will be coming back home to live."

I was sat at the table doing my homework when Uncle Will came home from work and headed to the bathroom to wash and change his clothes.

"What's the meaning of this, young lady?" he said, returning to the living room. I looked up wondering what I had done wrong.

"What's your coat doing on the bed? It should be hung up in the wardrobe."

I felt my face go bright red. "I'm... I'm sorry, Uncle Will," I stuttered.

"Make sure you hang it up in future," he told me. "I don't want Aunty Alice having to run around after you."

"I'm sorry, Uncle Will, I'll make sure I hang it up from now on."

I felt very hurt and finished my homework with my heart in my mouth. I was quiet at dinner and when Aunty Alice asked me what was wrong, I said I was tired and took myself off for an early night – making sure to be quick in the bathroom.

On the way to school the next morning, David and Sarah said they knew Aunty Alice didn't have a television and asked if I wanted to go to theirs at the weekend to watch Six-Five Special, a Saturday evening pop music programme. I decided to ask Aunty Alice that evening if I could go. She had mentioned Uncle Will would be out so the timing was good.

The day went by as usual and I was relieved to get good marks for my homework. "You're doing really well," Mr Sinclair told me. "You'll be ready for your new school later this year."

It suddenly hit me that this change was coming up fast. I hadn't thought about it and asked Sheila and Hazel what they were going to do.

"We'll have to catch the bus into town every day," said Hazel. "We'll get dropped off and collected outside the school gate so there's no need to worry."

"You'll have us for company," added Sheila. "We'll all be able to meet up and go in together."

Their words made me feel a bit better. Back at the bungalow, and with Uncle Will having gone out, I asked Aunty Alice about going to watch TV with Sarah and David. "That'll be fine," she said, before she got her sewing box out and showed me how she crocheted. She asked if I wanted to learn embroidery and showed me a chair-back she had embroidered herself.

"It's lovely," I said. "I'd love to learn."

"I'll get you some coloured silks next time we go shopping," she said. "You can practise on a dressing table runner I've not got around to doing. By the way, your father is coming up to see you on Sunday. He'll be able to tell you how your mother's getting on."

I was glad Uncle Will was out as Aunty Alice and I spent a lovely evening together. She sat and cuddled me as we listened to classical music on the radio.

"Mum used to like listening to The Bluebell Polka," I told her. "It was lovely seeing her dancing around the room."

"I'm fond of dance music, too," she said. "When we were younger we used to attend dances held in the village hall."

I sat listening intently to stories of Mum and Aunty Alice at the village dances, until it was time for bed.

I felt happier the following morning as I told Sarah and David that Aunty Alice had agreed I could go to theirs to watch television. That afternoon we had PE and were due to play netball. "Can't play on an empty stomach," said Aunty Mary as she served up a lunch of stew and dumplings. It must have done me the world of good because I scored twice.

After doing my homework that evening, Aunty Alice mentioned how she thought I should start wearing a bra. Uncle Will was in the room and I blushed. It hadn't occurred to me I might need a bra, and when it was time for bed I asked her why I needed one. She told me it was only right now that I was developing. I couldn't help thinking how much my life was changing. She tucked me in and gave me a kiss.

The sun was shining when I woke and I could hear the sound of music playing. I knew Aunty Alice must be up preparing breakfast. I went to the bathroom to get washed before getting dressed. When Aunty Alice saw me she looked very pleased.

"Have your breakfast, Christine, then we'll get ready to go into the village," she said. After eating I helped wash the dishes and fed Thomas while Aunty Alice got ready. It was still a bit chilly despite the sunshine, so I put on my gloves and wrapped my scarf around my neck. Aunty Alice fastened her coat up to the collar and we began walking briskly. I was looking forward to buying silks so I could do some embroidery. Once in the village square, Aunty Alice headed towards the haberdashery. It was lovely and warm in the shop and a nice lady shopkeeper welcomed us.

"What can I help you with today?" she asked.

"We are looking for coloured silks so Christine can learn to do embroidery," said Aunty Alice.

We were taken to a couple of stands which had different coloured silks on. I looked in amazement at all the beautiful colours and stood for so long staring that Aunty Alice had to help me choose. When we took the silks to the counter, Aunty Alice told the lady we needed to buy bras for me.

"We'd better measure her," she said, reaching for the tape measure. I felt a bit embarrassed as she put it around me.

"I thought it was about time she started wearing a bra," said

Aunty Alice.

"You're right," agreed the shopkeeper. "I've got some beginner bras that would be just right for her."

I looked at the bras that she brought to the counter and pointed to nice cotton lacy ones that looked very pretty. I tried them on, and as Aunty Alice paid she told me I needed to wear them, especially when I was doing PE.

We went to the newsagents' to get Uncle Will's Cornish Guardian, then on to the butcher's shop where Aunty Alice bought a joint of meat. "We'll have a lovely roast tomorrow," she said.

I caught hold of one handle of the bag and helped her carry it. "You're a lovely little helper," she said, her words reminding me of Mum.

"Did you say Dad's coming up tomorrow?" I asked.

"Yes, love, he's asked Mrs Lane to take care of your mother for an hour. We'll find out then what arrangements he's been making."

"I hope Sam and Tim will come back home," I told her.

"I expect they will," she said. "It'll work out, wait and see."

Back in the bungalow, Aunty Alice showed me how to embroider and I made good progress on a leaf, with Uncle Will admiring how neatly I was doing it. We had tea and it was soon time for me to head next door to watch Six-Five Special.

"You can leave the dishes to me," said Aunty Alice. "I expect you're keen to go next door with Sarah."

I threw my coat on and ran down the path, feeling quite excited and a little bit nervous. I needn't have worried as there was a warm welcome waiting for me. David took my coat. I said hello to their mother before Sarah beckoned me to sit next to her on the couch just in time for the programme start.

"The Six-Five Special's coming down the line, the Six-Five Special's right on time..." went the theme tune. I was on the edge of my seat. The music was lively and made me feel like dancing. We were glued to the screen. Dickie Valentine appeared and started singing.

"I can't wait to see Lonnie Donegan," said David.

"Me too," I agreed. "I love it when I hear him on Radio Luxembourg."

David nodded. Our eyes turned back to the television when we heard Petula Clark singing Baby Lover. Her voice was dreamy and I loved every minute. After she finished the camera zoomed in on the presenters, Pete Murray and Josephine Douglas. Pete Murray welcomed the famous King Brothers, who sang Hand me down my Walking Cane. I knew the song having heard it on the radio. I wanted to dance, but decided against it in case Sarah's mother wouldn't like it.

Lonnie Donegan came next with Grand Coulee Dam, one of my favourites. I loved the beat, and we all tapped our toes. We then watched as The King Brothers came on again with the Six-Five Jive. The show was filmed on a train, and it looked as if everyone onboard got up and started dancing.

"That was lovely, I really enjoyed it," I told Sarah. "Thank you for inviting me over."

"You'll have to come every week to see it," she said.

"I will," I said. "I wouldn't want to miss it."

"Will I see you tomorrow?" Sarah asked.

"My father's coming up so I don't think I'll be able to come over."

"I'll call for you on Monday morning then," she said.

I thanked Sarah's mother and left. Back at Aunty Alice's, she made me a cup of cocoa before bed while I told her how amazing the show had been.

* * *

I heard Dad's motorbike soon after breakfast. I jumped up and ran down to the gate to greet him.

"All right love?" he said.

"Yes," I said, opening the gate and watching as he put his bike on its stand. I could see he looked down in the dumps.

"How's Mum?" I asked. "Are Sam and Tim coming home to help?"

"Let's go inside and I'll tell you all about it."

Aunty Alice already had the kettle on. "How's things, Jack?" she asked.

"Not good. I've been to the bank and found my account is empty."

Aunty Alice gasped. "What do you mean empty, Jack?"

"It seems Ruby has spent everything entering the football pools. She was paying Horace Batchelor for tips thinking she would have a big win. I didn't realise Horace Batchelor had such a hold over her."

Dad looked very worried and I went to give him a cuddle.

"What about Sam and Tim? Have they agreed to come home

to help?" asked Aunty Alice. "It would be the answer to your problems."

He looked a bit brighter then. "Yes," he said, "They're both giving in their notice at work and coming back to Cornwall."

I felt hugely relieved. "Will I be able to come back home?" I asked.

"I'm afraid your mother isn't well enough yet," said Dad. "Better wait a while, love. You're all right here with Aunty Alice."

I was bitterly disappointed. "When can I come down to see her?" I asked.

"She's still far too poorly yet, love. I'll let you know when she's well enough to see you."

His words were like a knife in my heart.

"Show your father your sewing, Christine," suggested Aunty Alice. As I fetched my embroidery from the bedroom I heard Aunty Alice tell Dad about the bras she'd bought me.

"That's really kind of you, Alice," he said. "I'm afraid I can't afford to pay you at the moment."

"I understand. You've got enough problems to deal with."

He enjoyed looking at my embroidery, but soon said he needed to be getting back to relieve Mrs Lane.

"I feel sorry for Dad finding his bank account empty," I told Aunty Alice once he'd gone.

"It's grown up problems, love," she said. "Not for you to worry about."

"Yes, but I'm worried about how he will manage."

"You shouldn't be worrying about things like that." She gave me a hug. "Enjoy your childhood because you'll have grown-up problems soon enough."

Chapter Fourteen

MR SINCLAIR TOOK the register and noticed a boy called Tippett was missing. When he asked the class where the pupil was, someone called out, "He's gone scrumping apples, sir."

There was whispering at the back of the class until Mr Sinclair banged on his desk. "He's done what?" he bellowed. "Just wait until I get hold of him."

He jumped up and went to get Archibald, his cane, from the cupboard. Even though Mr Sinclair only caned boys and never girls, I was always frightened to see Archibald. Mr Sinclair whipped the air, making a loud swishing sound. "There he is, damn him!"

I looked through the window and saw Tippett munching away on an apple. Mr Sinclair rushed out of the classroom and dragged Tippett in by his ear.

"Where have you been, boy?" he demanded.

"I... I overslept, sir," stammered Tippett.

"Don't tell me lies boy! I know what you've been up to.

You've been scrumping apples."

"I... I was hungry, sir."

"That's no excuse," roared Mr Sinclair. "You've no right to pick other people's apples."

Poor Tippett looked terrified. "Hold your hands out, boy," ordered Mr Sinclair.

I thought Mr Sinclair was really horrid at times. I could see Tippett had tears in his eyes and it was difficult for him to stop himself from crying. Mr Sinclair gave him three swipes on each hand, before sending him to his seat. I couldn't help thinking how unfair it was. I knew Tippett wouldn't have been scrumping at all if he hadn't been hungry. I felt an injustice had been done and really hated Archibald, so I started hatching a plan.

I returned to the classroom at break time and took Archibald from the cupboard. It took all my strength, but when I heard Archibald snap I knew it had been worth it. I put the broken cane back in the cupboard and rushed back to my friends in the playground, who assumed I'd been to the toilet.

That night I fell asleep feeling nervous about what would happen when Mr Sinclair discovered Archibald. He looked furious when we filed into class the next morning.

"Who's had the audacity to break Archibald?" he screamed, bringing his ruler down on his desk. "Whoever did it had better own up."

I was terrified and kept quiet as Mr Sinclair's eyes fell on Tippett. The class was silent. "It was you wasn't it, Tippett?" he said, storming towards the boy and grabbing him by the ear. I knew then that I couldn't let an innocent person take the blame.

"It wasn't Tippett, Sir. It was me." My voice was barely audible as I looked down at the floor. "I broke Archibald, Sir."

"You did what?" shouted Mr Sinclair, dropping Tippett and taking hold of me. "Right, let's see what the headmaster has to say about this."

I was shaking and felt sick as he marched me down the corridor. The headmaster looked surprised. "I've found the culprit," Mr Sinclair told him. "It's hard to believe, but it was Christine who broke Archibald."

The headmaster looked at me over the rim of his glasses. "Never," he said. "I felt sure it was one of the boys." He got up. "What excuse have you got, young lady?"

"I'm sorry, Sir," I said. "I felt sorry for Tippett."

"Take your hands out of your pockets, girl, when you're talking to the headmaster," said Mr Sinclair. I did as I was told immediately. "What punishment should she be given, Headmaster?"

I was worried stiff as I waited for his answer. It seemed like an eternity before he put me out of my misery.

"One hundred lines to be written in my office," he said finally. "She can report to my office at break time."

"Agreed," said Mr Sinclair. "And if you think you've got rid of Archibald, Christine, you're wrong. I'll be bringing a new cane to school in the morning."

I felt my heart sink. I'd broken Archibald for nothing. At break time I went to the headmaster's office and began writing, 'I must not break Mr Sinclair's cane in the future.' The headmaster stayed in his office to keep an eye on me and I felt sad as I heard the others playing outside.

Everyone soon heard about Archibald and me, as well as Archibald the Second, who arrived in the classroom as soon as Mr Sinclair could manage.

David was very impressed and laughed when I confirmed it had been me who'd stood up to Mr Sinclair. "It's really lucky you're a girl," he told me. "Otherwise you'd be for the high jump. A hundred lines; that's getting away with it lightly."

"I feel sorry for Christine," Sarah told him.

"Please don't tell Uncle Will and Aunty Alice," I begged them.

"No, of course we won't," they said.

I felt better and hoped everyone would forget about it. I hadn't even thought that someone might tell Aunty Mary.

"What's this I hear about you breaking Archibald?" she asked when I went down the next day at lunchtime. I couldn't help blushing with embarrassment. "When I heard about it I thought you must have had a good reason."

We sat down to eat and I told her all about Tippett. "Now I understand," she said sympathetically.

"Please don't tell Aunty Alice" I asked.

"No, I won't, but I think you should tell her." I must have looked surprised. "It'll be better coming from you than for her to learn about it from someone else later."

I knew Aunty Mary was right but felt uncertain. "Tell her when Uncle Will has gone out," she said.

That evening I summoned all my courage and told Aunty Alice what I'd done. "Tippett only picked an apple because he was hungry," I explained.

"Sadly a lot of things in life aren't fair, my dear," she said.

I looked at her and could see she wasn't angry with me. When I went to bed that night she told me I was a good little girl and that my heart was in the right place.

Dad came over the following weekend with news that Sam and Tim would be home on Monday. It seemed Sam already had a job lined up and would be able to help out financially. I was desperate to go back and be a family again, but Dad said I should wait until the end of the summer holidays, which must have been four months away, maybe more. Mum was still paralysed and confined to bed – I hadn't seen her for six weeks.

"I was hoping to spend the summer holiday with Lucy again," I told Dad.

"Lucy's father's getting married again and the family are moving," Dad told me.

My face crumbled and I burst into tears. I'd been looking forward to spending time with her.

"Don't cry about it." Dad gave me a cuddle. "It'll be nice for Lucy and Liam."

"Yes," I said. "But I'll miss her, Dad. We had lots of fun last summer."

"I expect she'll keep in touch," Aunty Alice said gently. "You'll be able to spend the summer holiday with Sarah and David."

I was glad about that at least.

Aunty Alice took me to church that Sunday. I was looking forward to it as I hadn't been for ages. We were greeted by the vicar. "So nice to see that you've brought your niece," he said to my aunt before guiding us to a pew at the front.

It was all rather strange to me, but I liked it. We listened to the sermon and sang some hymns. I admired, once again, Aunty Alice's soprano voice with her sweet tones rising above all the other voices. I knew most of the hymns and felt happy to be able to join in. When the service was over Aunty Alice stopped to speak to some of her friends and seemed proud to introduce me. On the way home I told her I'd like to go with her to church every Sunday, and she was delighted.

Mr Sinclair was in a better mood the following morning and decided to tell us one of his stories. We listened for the umpteenth time to the one about his ship almost getting torpedoed.

"I would like to join the Navy, sir," Tippett shouted out.

Mr Sinclair looked surprised. "It's all right if you want to see the world," he told us. I could see some of the boys thinking about it. "No doubt some of you will work at the clay works and some will help run family farms. There are others, like Tippett, who may decide to join the Navy."

I'd never thought about what I wanted to do after leaving school. At break time I asked my friends if they'd given it any thought.

"I'd like to be a nurse," said Hazel, before Maureen told us she'd like a job in the bank.

"I'll help dad in the shop," added Sheila. "What do you want to do, Christine?"

"I'm not sure," I said. "But I know I'd like to get married and have children."

We all agreed we wanted to get married. By coincidence, when I arrived at The Jolly Miller that lunchtime, Aunty Mary told me she was going to marry Roy, her new man friend. I was surprised but could see that she was happy. Aunty Mary said it was going to be a small wedding and asked me to tell Aunty Alice, which I did. She was taken aback that she hadn't been told in person, but said she'd been expecting the news. When she told Uncle Will, he commented that Roy was a decent chap, that it had been hard for Mary since she lost Tom and that it would be nice for them to run the pub together.

At that moment I heard my father's motorbike pull up outside. He came into the house looking excited. "Your brothers have come home," he told me.

I was thrilled and immediately asked when I could go and see them. "This weekend, if it's all right," he said, looking at Aunty Alice.

"Yes, that'll be fine, we'll come down on Saturday afternoon," she told him.

He came in for a chat and a cup of tea, and Aunty Alice filled him in about Mary. My father knew Roy because he ran a smallholding and he and Mum had bought turkeys from him in the past.

The week couldn't go quickly enough for me. We were studying algebra at school. It was difficult, and when I told Aunty Alice I was struggling she suggested Sam might be able to help me and that I should take my homework when I saw him the next day.

I was so excited to be seeing my mother and brothers that I could hardly sleep. The sun was shining when I woke. Aunty Alice made me scrambled eggs and said we would take some grapes for my mother. "I know she can manage to eat a few without choking," she said to my surprise. "We'll peel them first, that will make them easier for her to swallow."

"I can do that," I said, "I can peel them for her." I wanted to do all I could to help her.

"Your mother's still quite poorly dear, so don't be upset when you see her," she said kindly. "She's getting better bit by bit, but she's still very poorly."

I felt sad. We got ready and I brushed my hair twice, wanting to look my best. I was in high spirits as we left the bungalow to buy grapes on the way to the bus stop.

* * *

As we turned the corner after I'd leapt from the bus, Fir Tree Cottage came into sight. I broke into a run and as I got to the gate Sam looked up from cleaning his bike, a huge grin spreading across his face. I opened the gate and ran towards him.

"My goodness you've grown up," he said, giving me a huge hug. "Where's my little sister?"

Aunty Alice caught me up. "Christine's a young lady now," she told him.

Sam looked amazed. "I won't be able to give you a bearding now," he said. I felt glad because I used to hate it. "Anyway, come on in. Tim's been waiting to see you."

Tim was sat at the table repairing a watch. I ran to him. He looked pleased to see me and explained to Aunty Alice that he'd found a good trade repairing watches and was going to start making rings. "I can do that while I'm staying at home looking after mother," he said.

Mother! I started up the stairs with Aunty Alice behind me. Just as I did, Dad came out of the bedroom to meet us. "Your mother's been waiting to see you, Christine," he said. "I'll make us all a cup of tea."

She was sitting up in bed, looking pale with her hair greyer than when I last saw her. I got on the bed beside her. "I'm here, Mum," I told her, cuddling into her with tears in my eyes.

She smiled a half smile which lifted my heart. Aunty Alice took the grapes out of her bag. "Would you like a seedless grape, Mum?" I asked.

She put her hand out as if to say she would. "Don't forget to peel them first, Christine," Aunty Alice reminded me.

I carefully peeled a grape and held it up to Mum's mouth. It seemed to take her ages to eat it, but she looked like she enjoyed it. I peeled another one. "You'd better not give her too many at once," Aunty Alice warned me. "Take it slowly."

I waited patiently as Mum ate the grape. Dad came in with the tea. "Christine's spoiling you, Ruby," he said as I put another grape in her mouth. He gave Aunty Alice a cup of tea and put mine on the table. Mum started coughing. "You'd better make that the last one," said Dad.

Once Mum had swallowed the grape, Dad went around to the side of the bed and propped her up with the pillows. He held the beaker of tea up to her mouth and she took a sip. "She's improving slowly," he told us.

"Sam couldn't believe how much Christine had grown," said Aunty Alice.

"Well, they've been away quite a while," said Dad.

"I'll be coming home to live again soon, Mum," I told her. Her eyes lit up.

"You'd better go down and see if Sam can help you with your homework," said Aunty Alice, taking my exercise book out of her bag. "She's learning how to do algebra, Jack."

"Oh, I see," said Dad, before calling down the stairs, "Can you give Christine a hand with her homework, Sam?"

"Yes," called Sam.

I went downstairs and Sam helped me. I was nearly finished when Aunty Alice came back down. "Come up and give your mother a kiss, we'll have to be leaving."

"Thanks, Sam," I said.

"That's all right." He gave me a wink. "You'll get top marks on Monday."

"It's the rest of the week I've got to worry about," I said. "We've got a test to see which class we'll go into at our new school. I hope I get to stay with my friends."

"You'll be fine," said Sam. "Just do your best."

I smiled as I went up the stairs and kissed Mum. "Love you, Mum," I said. "See you again soon."

We had to run for the bus and as I sat catching my breath I felt so happy that I'd seen everyone. "Well, things are falling into place," said Aunty Alice. "It will be nice when you can go home again and be with your family."

"I'm looking forward to it," I told her.

Chapter Fifteen

IT WASN'T LONG before it was my last lunch at The Jolly Miller. Bosun was waiting to greet me as always, and he amazed Aunty Mary by knowing what time I'd be there. Roy had provided a chicken for me to have a special roast on my last day. When it was time to leave, Aunty Mary made me promise I'd still visit her.

"Of course I will," I said.

"And me and Bosun," added Roy.

At the end of the school day all the teachers came in to wish us well. "Make sure you carry on working hard, Christine," Mr Sinclair told me. "You've done well this year."

I blushed. He made his way round the class giving everyone some good advice. "Let's hope you all take notice," he said at the end. At that moment the school bell rang. "Good luck, everyone!" were his final words.

I heard the familiar sound of chairs being pushed back and everyone leaving. I glanced back when I got to the door and felt a pang of sadness that I wouldn't be coming back to my village school anymore.

"Don't forget to meet up at the bus stop next term!" Sheila's voice broke into my thoughts.

"I won't forget," I called back.

"Neither will I," chorused Maureen and Hazel.

"Have a lovely holiday everyone," added Sheila.

I made my way to the gate to meet up with Sarah and David. "Mr Sinclair is not as bad after all," I told them. "He's been really nice to us all today."

"That's because we're leaving," laughed David. "He's glad to get rid of us"

"You're awful, David, you liked him really," Sarah told him.

"Yes, I suppose you're right," he admitted. "It's because of him I want to join the Navy."

"Surprisingly enough so does Tippett," I said.

"Are you coming round to watch Six-Five Special?" Sarah asked as we arrived at my gate.

"Yes, I'll see you tomorrow," I called out as I ran up the path.

The summer holidays were fun. Dad had called round on the first Sunday, telling us how things were easier with the boys at home and that Mum was a lot happier.

"That's good," said Aunty Alice. "It won't be long before Christine joins you."

"That'll make Ruby even happier," said Dad.

I spent time with Sarah and David during the week and we always watched Six-Five Special on Saturdays.

"We'd better get your school uniform tomorrow," Aunty Alice told me one evening. "You'll be going to your new school in a couple of weeks. And your father wants you to return home next week. Your mother and brothers want you back home too."

"Yes," I said. "I hadn't realised it would be so soon." I must have looked a bit downcast as she put her arm around me.

"I know, dear," she told me. "But it's all for the best."

I made an excuse to go to my bedroom. I wanted to be alone. I realised that now the time had come, I didn't really want to go back. I had memories of going hungry and there being no food in the cupboard. I tried to brush these thoughts aside. I knew in my heart of hearts that I had been longing to return home to live with Mum.

I was feeling very confused about it all when Aunty Alice looked in the door. "What's wrong, dear?" she asked.

"I don't want to go home, I don't want to leave you," I said.

She put her arm around me. "I know how you feel, dear. I don't want you to go either." I began to cry. "Please don't cry," she said, handing me a tissue. "I understand that you've been happy and feeling quite settled here. But it was never meant to be permanent. It's only natural that your family want you back."

"I suppose so," I said, doing my best to put on a brave face.

"Everything will work out," she reassured me.

We went into town the following day to buy my school uniform. Dad called up to see me at the weekend. "Aunty Alice will bring you back home on Wednesday," he told me. "She's given me your new school uniform and I'll take it home with me."

I nodded. "Is there anything else I can take?" he asked Aunty Alice. "I don't want you to have too much to carry on the bus"

She looked through my wardrobe and gave him some more

clothes.

"I'll get Mrs Lane to make up that bed I got you at the auction," said Dad as he was about to leave.

"Thanks, Dad."

He gave me a hug and started up his bike. "We're looking forward to having you home," he called out before riding off.

* * *

A feeling of apprehension came over me as I got dressed on the morning I was to return home. Again, I couldn't help thinking of the times I'd felt hungry and disappointed to open the cupboards and find them empty. I did my best to brush bad thoughts aside, but they wouldn't go away. I began to feel a bit panicky and unsure about leaving Aunty Alice. I tried to convince myself not to be so silly, that things would be different now my brothers were home again. I did my best to look happy as I sat down at the table for breakfast. Aunty Alice didn't look very happy either.

"Poached eggs on toast, Christine. A little treat before you go," she said as she put my plate on the table. "We'll have a nice cup of tea, too. Can't beat a cup of tea to start the day."

I felt a lump in my throat and found it hard to swallow.

"Are you all right, Christine?" she asked.

"I had a problem swallowing my toast," I told her. "I thought I was about to choke."

I managed my toast knowing it would please Aunty Alice to see an empty plate. I finished my cup of tea and went to help with the dishes.

"Could I feed Thomas before I go?" I asked.

"Yes of course, dear," she said. "He's bound to miss you feeding him, isn't he?"

I nodded. She opened the cat food and I fought back the tears as she handed it to me.

"Here, Thomas," I said, putting it down for him to eat. After Thomas finished eating I sat stroking him for a while.

Aunty Alice and I caught the bus. As we went past the council houses I looked to see if any of my friends were outside playing.

Aunty Alice must have seen me looking. "They may have gone into town to buy new school clothes," she said.

"That's possible," I agreed.

"I've got pasties for your tea," she said, looking down at her bag. "I expect your father, Sam and Tim will be glad of that."

"What about Mum?" I asked. "Is there one for her?"

"I've made her a vegetable one. We'll be able to mash it up for her."

Any doubts I had about returning vanished and I found myself running ahead so I could get there quicker. Sam was in the driveway and I ran into his arms. "It's great to have you home again," he said giving me a hug. "Mother's been waiting for you. She'll be delighted."

I went into the cottage and said hello to Tim before rushing upstairs. Dad heard us coming and was out on the landing to greet us.

"Ruby's been getting quite excited," he said to Aunty Alice. "She's been waiting for a cuddle from you, Christine."

I was pleased to see my mother looking a lot brighter. She

held her arms out to me and I got on the bed and we had a lovely cuddle. I felt happy to be home and kissed her on the cheek.

"It's so much better with the boys back," Dad told us. "And now Christine's home, Ruby's happiness is complete."

"It's nice for the family to be back together," said Aunty Alice.

Dad wanted to show me my bedroom and the bed he'd bought at the auction. Mrs Lane had made it up as promised, even putting flowers on my dressing table.

"Aren't they pretty?" said Aunty Alice, as I went over to take a sniff.

"Roses are my favourite, they smell gorgeous," I said.

Dad smiled. "Mrs Lane has hung up all your clothes in the wardrobe."

"It looks like a real welcome home for you, Christine," said Aunty Alice.

After looking through my clothes, we went back in to see Mum. "Did you like your room?" she asked, her voice slurred. I felt overwhelmed to hear her speak after she hadn't been able to talk for so long.

"It's lovely," I said. "I'm happy to be home."

"I've made you a vegetable pasty," Aunty Alice told her. "I was thinking if we mash the vegetables up you might be able to eat some."

Mum smiled.

"Thanks, Alice, I'm sure Ruby will give it a try," said Dad.

"I haven't had a pasty in ages," said Mum faintly.

When it was time for Aunty Alice to go, she gave Mum a

goodbye kiss. I followed her downstairs and stopped while she said goodbye to my brothers. "Enjoy your pasties," she told them as she walked out the door.

I followed her to the gate. "Make sure you let me know how you get on at school," she said.

"I will," I assured her. I stood watching until she reached the corner. She turned around and we waved to each other before she disappeared out of sight.

Back inside, Sam and Tim had started eating their pasties. "Sit down and have your pasty," said Sam, pointing to the chair beside him.

"Home didn't seem like home without our little sister," he continued as I sat down.

I spent as much time as I could with Mum that day, telling her about school, my friends and the summer holidays as she smiled her half smile and nodded at what I said.

At bedtime Dad gave me some matches. "I've put a candle in the candlestick beside your bed," he said.

I walked along the landing and into my room. I thought how soft the bed looked and how nice it would be to sleep in. I couldn't wait to pull the sheets back as soon as I had put my nightdress on. I sank into the feather mattress relishing its softness, and I must have fallen asleep within a few minutes.

The next morning it dawned on me gradually that I was back at home. I couldn't hear anyone and remembered that my brothers were going to look at a van Tim wanted to buy. I got dressed and went in to see Mum. She was sleeping peacefully so I didn't wake her.

I went downstairs and was pleased to find cornflakes on the table. I found Dad had put a bottle of milk chilling in a bowl of cold water. I poured the milk onto my cornflakes and sprinkled on a spoonful of sugar. After I'd finished my breakfast I went outside to look at my bike; I hadn't ridden it for ages and decided to give it a clean.

When I opened up the door of the shed I was surprised to find my bike wasn't there. I was trying to think where else Dad could have put it when I heard Sam's motorbike coming down the road. I closed the shed door and ran over to meet him. I climbed on the bar of the gate so I could look over just in time to see Sam pull up outside. Tim pulled up behind in what was obviously his new van. "It goes well," he told Sam. "Flies up the hills, I can tell you."

"How's Mum?" Sam asked me.

"She's fast asleep. I thought it best not to wake her up."

Sam looked worried. "She's been sleeping a lot recently. I'll nip up and take a look."

He took off his jacket and gloves and went indoors. Tim and I followed. "She's still sleeping," Sam told us when he came back down again. "Dad said she needs plenty of rest to get better."

"She'll bang on the ceiling with her stick if she needs us," said Tim.

Tim started talking about the van he'd bought when I suddenly remembered I couldn't find my bike. "Do you know what Dad's done with my bike?" I asked. "I was going to give it a clean but couldn't find it in the shed."

I could see by their faces they weren't sure what to say.

"Dad's given it away," Sam told me reluctantly.

"He said that you'd got too big for it so gave it to Mrs Lane for her daughter," added Tim.

I was really upset. "I expect he'll get you another," said Sam. "Stop looking so upset, cheer up. You can come out for a ride in the van with us this afternoon."

Dad came home soon after. "Why did you give my bike away to Mrs Lane?" I asked him. He looked flustered and took time to reply.

"I thought you'd got too big for it," he said apologetically. "You hadn't used it for a while and I didn't think you wanted it anymore."

Before I had a chance to protest Sam and Tim came running out, keen to show him the new van. Dad looked glad to have a distraction. He looked over the van then told me to see if Mum was awake and would like a cup of tea. I went upstairs and was pleased to find her awake.

"Dad's home, Mum," I said. "He wants to know if you'd like a cup of tea."

She gave me a half smile and nodded her head. "Sam and Tim have bought a van," I told her. "They're taking me out with them this afternoon. I'll let Dad know you want a cup of tea."

Later that afternoon I went out with my brothers to Sam's old RAF base. On the way back we stopped at a garage where Sam bought me some wine gums. Tim started up the engine and we joined the traffic again. Sam opened a packet of cigarettes and lit one. "I needed that," he said, inhaling deeply before blowing smoke through his mouth.

"It's a waste of money if you ask me," said Tim as some of the smoke drifted back towards me and I started coughing.

"Let's get some fresh air in here," said Tim, opening the window.

"For goodness sake, stop fussing," Sam told him. "Keep your eyes on the road so we don't miss the turning."

"Keep your eyes open then," said Tim. "You know this road better than me."

"Isn't it lovely seeing all the green grass again after living in London for ages?" Sam asked Tim.

"It's all right, I suppose."

We passed the garage where Sam had hired cars to take us all out, and he said how he wished we would do that again. Then he spotted someone he knew. "That was George back there. Stop the van. I want to get out and see him."

Tim pulled over and Sam jumped out. "I won't be long," he called back.

I looked out the back window and could see them talking. Tim didn't look very pleased.

"Have you got any sweets left?" he asked, turning to me.

"There's two left, you can have them."

He took the bag. "I suppose I'm lucky to have any," he said in an annoyed tone.

Sam was soon climbing back in the van. "I've found out some interesting news," he told us. "You'll never believe it, Tim."

On the way home we passed a school and I remembered that I would be starting school the following week. I wasn't listening to Sam telling Tim what he'd heard from George, but I did hear

Tim say, "Never. That's hard to believe."

"It's true all right. George has got the proof," Sam assured him.

We were just about to pull onto the main road, which was very busy. "It's these bloody Sunday afternoon drivers," said Tim angrily. "A lot of them shouldn't be on the road."

He suddenly put his foot down and started overtaking. I was frightened. "Don't go so fast, Tim," I told him.

"Shut up, you're just a kid," he retorted angrily as I clung to my seat. "Why don't you move over, you blithering idiot?"

"Mind out, Tim, there's a motorbike coming," yelled Sam.

I looked up in time to see a motorbike heading towards us from the opposite direction. "Get back in," Sam shouted. Tim ignored him. Sam attempted to grab the steering wheel, but it was too late. There was a bang and I felt the van shake as the motorbike collided with the wing.

"You idiot, see what you've done!" Sam shouted.

"He should have been looking where he was going," Tim shouted back.

The motorbike rider was lying on the grass verge with his bike beside him. "We'd better go over and see if he's all right," said Sam.

I was really worried and followed them. As we got closer I realised who it was and felt my heart sink. "Oh no, it's Roy," I heard myself saying. "It's Aunty Mary's husband."

Sam looked dismayed, but Tim was smirking.

"Are you all right, Roy?" Sam asked.

He opened his eyes and looked up. "I think so," he said, "just a bit shaken. Can you help me up?"

Sam caught hold of his arm and helped him to his feet. "What happened?" asked Roy.

"Just a little mishap, you hit the wing of our van," said Sam.

"Well, I seem all right, how's my motorbike?"

Sam picked up the bike and started it. "It looks okay, no real harm done," said Roy. "Thankfully I landed on some grass."

A few cars had stopped by now, but they moved on once Roy got up and said he wasn't injured.

"Will you be all right, Roy?" I asked, looking at the grazes on his face.

He smiled at me. "It'll take more than that to hurt a tough old bird like me," he said. "Anyway, how's your mother, Christine?"

"She's improving slowly," I told him.

"I'm glad to hear it." He dusted off his oil skins. "Well, I'd better get back to Mary. She'll wonder where I am."

Sam helped him get his bike back on the road.

"Go careful, Roy," Tim called out. Roy gave us a wave.

"My God, how embarrassing," said Sam as we watched him ride away.

"What can I say to Aunty Mary?" I asked. "She's bound to be annoyed."

"You'd better keep away from them for a while," said Tim sharply.

"I'm sure she'll realise it was an accident," said Sam as we got back in the van. "Let's get home for our tea"

I sat quietly in the back, upset by what had happened. "Are you all right Christine?" Sam asked when I got out.

"I feel a bit shook up."

"Have your tea and then get off to bed," he said. I gave a little smile. "It'll all seem much better after a good night's sleep," he added.

That night I found it impossible to sleep as I kept seeing Roy hitting the van with his bike. I was wondering why Tim had kept overtaking and knew we wouldn't have had the accident if he hadn't. It had been a really strange day. I couldn't understand why Tim had insisted I keep away from Aunty Mary.

I woke to the sound of Mrs Lane talking to Mum. I realised Dad must have gone to work and that she'd arrived to take care of her. I got dressed and went in to see to see them.

"It's great to have you back home again, Christine" said Mrs Lane when she saw me. "I know how much your mother was missing you."

"It's good to be home again," I told her.

As I made my way downstairs I heard Sam say, "Do you mean you knew it was Roy before you hit him?"

"Yes, of course I did. I wanted to teach the old bugger a lesson," laughed Tim.

"You're bloody stupid, Tim. You could easily have killed him." Sam sounded horrified.

"Christine's here, she wants her breakfast," said Tim as he looked up and saw me. "For goodness sake, Sam, keep your mouth shut."

Sam went quiet.

"Do you want some cornflakes?" asked Tim.

"Yes please," I said as I sat down. Tim tipped cornflakes in my bowl and poured on some milk.

"You didn't hear what we were talking about did you, Christine?" asked Sam.

"No, I didn't," I replied, thinking it was the best thing to say.

"Just Tim, talking a load of old rubbish anyway," said Sam. "You wouldn't say anything anyway would you, Christine?"

I had started eating my cornflakes so just shook my head. "That's a good girl." Sam patted me on the shoulder. I ate my breakfast and went back upstairs to see Mum.

"So, I hear you're starting your new school tomorrow," Mrs Lane said.

"Yes," I replied. "I feel a bit nervous about it though."

"Have you seen Tim's new van?" Mum asked her.

"Not really, I just noticed it when I came in," said Mrs Lane.

As Mrs Lane was leaving she mentioned the van to Tim. "It looks all right but it's a pity about the dent in the wing," she said.

Tim blushed. I was just going to tell her about the accident when he gave me a threatening glance. "I managed to get the price knocked down because of it," he told her. "Sam's mate's a panel beater so he'll soon put it right."

When Mrs Lane had gone, I asked Tim, "How am I going to get up to the village to catch the school bus? I didn't expect Dad to give away my bike."

"Don't worry, I'll drop you up in the van. I'll be able to collect you after school as well."

"Will you? It would be good if you could."

"Of course, I've got to look after my little sister."

Dad returned home and I went upstairs with him so I could

spend as much time as I could with Mum. Then I needed to sort out my uniform and have a good wash before school started the following day.

After tea I asked Dad if he could help wash my hair. He looked over at Tim. "You could help Christine wash her hair couldn't you, Tim? Mother used to do it."

"I'll give it a go," said Tim.

"Thanks, son. I'll wash the dishes and you help Christine."

"I suppose it'll end up being my job every week."

"You don't mind helping your little sister, do you?"

"No, it'll be all right."

Tim put the kettle on while I got the plastic bowl and shampoo. "It's not easy washing your hair in a plastic bowl," he said as he was rinsing the soap suds off. "Here, let's help dry it."

He started rubbing my hair with a towel. "Thanks Tim," I said when it was done.

"It's all right, I'll be able to help you every week."

I gave my mother a kiss and went to bed.

Chapter Sixteen

"TIME TO GET up, Christine." Tim gave me a shake and I opened my eyes. "Hurry up and get dressed," he said, leaving my room and leaving me to wonder what my new school would be like.

"Hurry up, Christine!" called Tim's voice again.

"I'm nearly ready, just brushing my hair," I called. I was a mix of nerves and excitement. I checked my appearance in the mirror, picked up my satchel and went in to see Mum. She was sleeping so I made my way downstairs where Tim gave me cornflakes and a cup of tea.

"I was going to say goodbye to Mum but she's fast asleep," I told him.

"It's best not to wake her," he said. "You can tell her about your new school when you get home."

I nodded, finished my breakfast and followed Tim out to the van. When we arrived in the village I could see other children waiting for the bus. "My friends are here," I told him. "I'll go over and join them."

"Wait a minute," he said. "Dad's given me your dinner money." Tim handed me the money – it hadn't occurred to me, having eaten at Aunty Mary's pub for so long.

"I expect Dad will find it harder now he has to pay for your school dinners," said Tim. This worried me but I knew there was nothing I could do about it. The bus soon arrived, and as I joined my friends, Tim spoke to the driver before telling me he'd collect me at 4.30. I sat beside Hazel, and Maureen got on and sat behind us. "Where's Sheila?" I asked them.

"I don't suppose you've heard, have you?" said Hazel. "Her Dad found another job so they've left the village. She's going to a new school."

"Oh no," I said. I felt really sad and wondered if I'd ever see her again.

"Lucky her, though," said Maureen. "She's living near the beach."

I was glad for Sheila but knew I'd miss her.

Maureen, Hazel and I chatted on the short journey about whether we'd be in the same class; we hoped so. And when we pulled up, the school looked huge.

"I'm going to get lost," said Hazel, her voice suddenly sounding small.

Maureen was much more cheerful. "Don't worry, we'll soon get used to it," she said.

A prefect approached us and introduced herself as Mary. She'd been given the job of showing round all the children arriving from our old school.

"Get in line then, two at a time," she said. I made sure I was beside Hazel and, once we were organised, Mary led the way.

"Where are we going?" I whispered to Hazel.

"I think I heard her say the assembly hall."

As we walked down a long corridor I was surprised to see classrooms on both sides. "There are loads of classes," Hazel whispered. "I wonder which one we'll be in."

Mary showed us into the huge assembly hall. "Welcome to your new school everyone." I looked up at the stage and saw a tall man speaking. "My name is Mr Smith and I'm the headmaster."

He was an imposing looking man. "I've brought you into the hall so we can sort out which class you're going to be in," he continued. "It'll depend on the results of the test you took at your previous schools."

A group of teachers came over and one of them asked for my name. When I told her, she said, "Well, Christine. You did well in the test, so you're going into the A stream." I was pleased. "Wait a few minutes and I'll get a prefect to take you to your class."

As I stood waiting, I realised Maureen and Hazel had already gone. Mary came over and led me back along the corridor to one of the many doors. "Your teacher is Mrs Wilson," she said. "You'll like her. She's really nice."

I started to feel less anxious until she opened the door of Mrs Wilson's class. "Good morning, Mrs Wilson," she said. "This is Christine, another new pupil for you. Where do you want her to sit?"

Mrs Wilson looked at me. "You're not very tall, Christine, so it might be best if you sit near the front," she said, pointing towards an empty seat.

I walked over and sat down. "You'll take Christine under your wing won't you, Wendy?" she asked the girl sitting next to me. "She's one of the new pupils joining our school today because their village school has stop taking seniors"

Wendy smiled and said she would. Then I listened carefully as Mrs Wilson read out the register. I wanted to learn everyone's name.

When the register was complete, Mrs Wilson walked round the class giving out books. "You're bound to find it a bit strange at first," she told me. "There's a different teacher for each subject so you'll have to change classes quite a lot. Wendy will take care of you and show you where to go."

At lunchtime Wendy took me to the canteen. It was so big I couldn't find Hazel or Maureen. The food was delicious – cottage pie, with jam tart and custard for afters. Wendy gave me a bit more of a tour after our meal and we went into the playground to continue looking for Hazel and Maureen, but they were nowhere to be seen. "I'll have to wait and see them on the bus," I told Wendy as the bell rang.

"You'll be able to arrange to meet them once you all know your way around," she said. I could tell she was trying to cheer me up. "We all have the same problem when we are new."

That afternoon Mrs Wilson gave us our timetables before we had geography, followed by maths. I did well and the teacher was pleased with me. Wendy joked that I'd be able to help her as maths was her worst subject. I said I'd be glad to.

I was desperate to see Hazel and Maureen, to hear how their

day had gone, and thrilled when I got on the bus to see they'd saved me a seat next to them. We shared our news. They were together in the same class, which made me sad. Maureen said it was good that I was in the top stream but I said I'd rather be with them, which was true.

Tim met me from the bus and when I got home I raced upstairs to tell Mum about my day. She was sitting up in bed with Dad beside her.

"How did you get on?" he asked.

"Quite well, I'm in the A stream."

They both looked pleased. "That's the top stream isn't it?" asked Dad.

"Yes" I said proudly.

"You've got a clever girl here, Ruby."

I gave Mum a kiss. "Sam did well at school so he'll be pleased to hear that," added Dad. I told Mum about Wendy, my new teachers and what I'd had for lunch. She looked interested and pleased all had gone well on my first day.

Back downstairs, Tim told Dad and me about some moulds he'd bought for jewellery making. "They arrived today," he said. "I'll be able to make rings to sell."

Dad and I went over to take a look. "Do you like them?" he asked. "As you can see they're made of wax." They were pink and I liked the colour. "I'll be able to get into business now."

"That's great, Tim," said Dad. "Quite ingenious, I'm sure you'll do well."

Tim smiled. "I'll take Christine with me when I go to sell them."

"I'd love to," I said.

Sam came home and was really pleased I'd made the A stream. He sat at the table and the four of us ate tea together.

"Do you fancy a bit of target practise after we've eaten?" Sam asked Tim.

Yep, I suppose we could. I want to get more practice with the .45."

I didn't know what they were talking about. "You can set up the targets for us after tea," Tim told me.

I looked puzzled. "Just collect as many tin cans as you can and line them up on the wall," he explained.

"I think you'll find some in the wash house, Christine," added Sam.

I was pleased to be able to help, so after I'd finished eating and drinking my tea, I went to set up the cans. Sam and Tim followed me outside.

"That's right, line them up," said Tim. When I glanced over I could see my brothers polishing a gun each.

"They're not real guns, are they?" I asked.

"Of course they are," Tim snapped. "Sam's is a .38 and mine's a .45. I could blow a man's head off with this." I shuddered. "But you've got to keep your mouth shut about it," he said, waving the gun in the air. He sounded angry.

"I won't say anything."

Dad called me in to get ready for bed and I was glad to go. He had a bowl of water ready for me so I could take it up and wash in my room. I made my way upstairs and went in to say goodnight to Mum. I kissed her. "Goodnight, Mum, I love you loads," I said.

"Goodnight, love." Her words were barely audible but they sounded wonderful to me. I blew her a kiss as I closed the door and went to my room. I could hear my brothers firing bullets in the back yard and whooping each time they hit a target. Tim's words about blowing a man's head off replayed in my head. I couldn't understand why they wanted guns or why they had brought them home.

* * *

Back in school the following morning, Mrs Wilson praised me for an essay I wrote about what I did during the summer holidays. At lunchtime Wendy introduced me to her friends Jenny, Janet, Heather and Joyce. They were really nice to me and we chatted away until the bell rang. I hadn't seen Hazel and Maureen again and we worked out on the bus home that they must have been getting changed for games, since the timing seemed to be staggered. When I got home that evening my mother was happy to hear that Wendy and I were becoming friends.

After tea, Tim said Sam was going to give him a hand making rings.

"Isn't that nice, Christine, you'll be able to see how it is done."

"It sounds interesting," I said, trying to please him.

He smiled. "You're welcome to stay and watch," he said. "You'll have to keep your distance, mind, as the fire will be red hot." I must have looked confused because he added, "That's so we can melt the gold."

By this point I was intrigued. Sam came in and went over to the Cornish range and started stoking the fire. "I've put more coal on, it should be blazing in a few minutes," he told Tim.

I sat in mother's chair which was closer to the fire. "You'd better move the chair back a little," said Sam. "There could be sparks."

"Here's the bellows, Sam," said Tim as he handed them over. I watched as Sam pumped the bellows furiously and the fire began to roar.

"That should do it," said Tim. "Now let's see if we can get it hot enough to melt the metal."

As I looked on, amazed, he put a pot on the fire. "How's it going?" Sam asked.

"Almost, not far off," said Tim.

"I hope so, pumping these bellows is hard work." Sam was sweating and out of breath by this point.

"That's it!" Tim shouted suddenly. Sam stopped pumping and I moved back as Tim lifted the pot off the fire and poured the melted gold into the moulds. "I'm glad that went all right," he said gleefully.

Sam wiped his brow and grinned. "I need some water."

Tim turned to me. "So, what did you think of that then?"

"All right," I said, unsure of what I should say.

"It'll be more than all right once I've made the rings. Wait and see."

I nodded. "Well, I'd better go up and see Mum like I promised," I said.

"Okay," said Tim. Sam came back into the room, then.

"Christine's not too impressed at the moment," Tim told him. "But she will be when they're done. Just wait until the platinum settings and gemstones are fitted."

Sam winked at me.

Chapter Seventeen

WENDY AND I were best friends by the end of that first week and she invited me to go to Saturday-morning cinema with her. I really wanted to go, but I knew I'd have to ask Dad.

Tim seemed tense when he collected me from the bus that evening. "I've got Mother's tea ready. You can give it to her when you get home."

"All right, I don't mind," I said. "I was going up to see her anyway."

"You'll have to do a lot more to help out now you're getting older," he said sharply.

"I know. I'll do my best to help out."

He turned to look at me, his face twisted with annoyance. "You can give her the bed pan when she needs it next," he spat. "You can't expect to always leave it to me."

"I know," I said quietly. "But I don't know what to do and I've never been asked."

Tim's voice dripped with sarcasm. "Well it's about time you

learnt then, isn't it?"

As soon as I got indoors, I took Mum's tea up to her. "I've got your tea, Mum," I said as I walked in. Her eyes lit up.

"Thanks, dear," she managed to say as I put the tray down on the dressing table.

"I'd better help you sit up first." I did my best to plump up her pillows and sit her up in bed to make it easier for her to swallow. "Just a little bit at a time, Mum," I said as she managed to swallow some. "You're doing well, Mum," I said encouragingly. I was so pleased when the plate was finally empty. "That's good," I told her. "Time for a nice drink of tea."

She looked grateful as I held the beaker to her lips. "That was nice," she said, sounding a bit out of breath.

I gave her a kiss. "Do you need the bed pan, Mum?"

She looked surprised. "Isn't Tim going to do it?"

I shook my head. "No, Mum, it's about time I tried to help you."

She nodded as if she understood. I got the pan from under the bed and tried to slide it under her bottom. I found it much harder than I thought it would be because of her paralysis. She tried lifting herself but I could see she couldn't do it. I was determined not to have to ask for Tim's help and struggled until I managed it. Mum looked relieved.

"Thanks, love, I've finished," she said after a while. I had problems getting the bed pan out from underneath her, not having realised how difficult it would be once it was full.

"Take care, love," she said once I'd done it. "Go careful now."

"It's all right, Mum, I can manage."

I took the bed pan away to empty it. "There we are, Mum. I managed all right," I said when I came back. She smiled at me.

"I'll go down and have my tea now and come up again later."

While I was eating, Sam came in and asked what food there was.

"Not much," I told him. "I've just had some soup."

He looked annoyed. "What's up with the old man? Why doesn't he make sure there's food in?"

"I don't know," I said, not wanting to criticise Dad.

"I suppose I'll have to go up to the shops if I want something," said Sam. "Need anything, Tim?"

"You could bring back a loaf of bread," he said.

There was a moment's silence after the sound of Sam's motorbike died away, then Tim exploded: "Where's that bloody screw gone?" he yelled. "You knocked it off the table, Christine."

"I... I didn't," I stammered, my words making him even more furious.

"You must have done. It was there a few minutes ago. You'd better get under the table and look for it."

I was terrified and quickly got down onto the floor, frantically searching for the screw. "Have you found it yet?" he shouted. "This watch won't be any good if you can't find it."

I could tell by the way he spoke that I would be in a lot of trouble if I didn't find it. I spotted something shiny and picked it up. "I think I've found it, Tim," I said, getting out from under the table and handing it to him.

"That's it. I knew you'd knocked it off the table!"

"I didn't think I did."

"You're so bloody clumsy."

There was no point arguing. I went upstairs and stayed with Mum until Dad came home. She didn't seem to realise Tim had been shouting at me; she was used to the sound of my brothers raising their voices.

* * *

I didn't get to go to the cinema that Saturday. The following day, Dad was on night shift and Sam decided to go out, so I asked Tim if he would help wash my hair again. He agreed, and I got a wooden chair to put the bowl on and filled it with warm water.

"Let's get on with it then," he said, picking up the shampoo. I bent over the bowl before Tim poured the shampoo on my head and began rubbing it into lather. I was used to him washing my hair but things seemed different this time. He started pressing himself up against me, which he'd never done before. I could feel something hard inside his trousers and didn't know what it was.

After he'd finished washing my hair he suddenly ordered me to go upstairs and get undressed. His words came as a total shock to me. He looked quite menacing and I was terrified. I knew something was very, very wrong.

"Please don't make me get undressed, Tim, I don't want to do it," I begged.

"Go upstairs right away and get undressed," he repeated. "If you don't, I will kill you and our mother. Is that what you want?"

I didn't want my brother to see me with no clothes on, so I begged and pleaded with him not to make me get undressed. He came towards me and hit me, then pushed me up the stairs. I could barely make it as my legs were weak and I shook with fear. I stood in my room too afraid to get undressed. I was petrified of what would happen. Tim followed, threatening me in a low voice to do exactly what he wanted or he'd kill me, and then kill Mum.

Taking my clothes off was the last thing I wanted to do, and I felt as if I might vomit. But there was no one in the house to help me and Mum was extremely vulnerable. The words Tim uttered about blowing a man's head off with his gun raced through my mind as I cried. I begged him to stop but this just made him more aggressive.

Once I was undressed, he inspected my body and looked at my private parts. Then he touched me. I cringed and waited until it was over. When he'd finished doing the things he wanted to do, he lay down on the bed beside me and stared into my eyes. "If you dare tell anyone about what's happened, I'll kill you and mother as well," he hissed. I nodded. "You know I mean it, don't you?"

"Yes," I said.

"You know if anyone heard the gun shots they wouldn't take any notice, don't you? They'd only think it was someone out shooting rabbits."

He continued to stare at me. He didn't seem to be blinking at all. "And it's no good you thinking of telling Aunty Alice and Uncle Will either," he sneered. "Because I'd go up there and kill them too. I'll make sure there's a family bloodbath if you dare open your mouth. I'd have to kill father and Sam as well."

I was barely breathing by now and my heart was beating so hard I felt it might rip through my chest. Tim laughed. "Don't think for one minute I wouldn't do it," he said. There was madness in his eyes.

Then suddenly he spoke as if nothing had happened. "You'd better get off to sleep now," he said. "I'll call you in the morning. I'll go in and give Mother the bed pan."

I lay in bed with my stomach churning, unable to stop the events replaying in my mind. Had that really just happened? I was shocked by Tim's threats, my mind in turmoil. I was terrified and scared for my life and for my mother's life. I realised that Tim, after staring at me in the way he did, was dangerous. He wasn't right in the head. I was just 12 years old and wouldn't be 13 for another two months. I knew nothing about sex and wasn't aware at the time that what he had just done was a crime. But I knew it made me feel ill. I knew I hated it. And I instinctively knew my brother shouldn't be doing it. I had no idea what to do or where to turn, petrified by his horrible threats which I felt sure he would carry out if I were to tell anyone.

Every sound made my heart race. I was terrified Tim would come back upstairs or go into my mother's room and hurt her. I eventually fell asleep and woke early, anxious to be dressed when Tim called me. He seemed surprised by that when he came in to say my breakfast was ready.

I knew it was important for me to behave normally and to act as if nothing had happened. I was desperate for him to take me to the bus stop so I could go off to school. I knew that was the only way I could get away from him.

"At least the old man's bought some cornflakes," he said as he passed me my bowl. "I think he heard Sam complaining about there being nothing in the cupboard."

I nodded, before quickly eating my breakfast. "I'm ready to go," I told him once I'd cleaned my teeth.

"Come on then," he said, jangling the van keys as usual. We got in the van and he started up and drove away. "Don't you dare tell anyone about what happened last night, mind," he said. "I meant what I said, so don't forget it."

I shuddered with fear. "I won't be saying anything."

"I'll pick you up tonight," he said before driving off, leaving me to breathe a sigh of relief.

Both Hazel and Maureen commented on how pale and tired I looked that morning on the bus. I couldn't concentrate on my lessons and the only moment of respite I found was when we sang Morning Has Broken in assembly. The words were a comfort to me. I looked at my friends and the adults around me, the teachers and canteen staff. I desperately wanted to tell someone what had happened, but I was too scared.

"You're not saying much," said Wendy at lunch. Her words brought me back to reality.

"Just worrying about my mother," I said.

Wendy looked surprised. "Why?" she asked. "Isn't she very well?"

I told Wendy about Mum's strokes. She was very sympathetic as her grandmother had experienced the same thing. It was nice to know she understood. "How bad is she?" she asked.

"She's bedridden and paralysed down one side," I said, just managing not to burst into tears.

"Oh dear, that's a shame. I do hope she gets better."

"I do too," I said as we finished our lunch.

"Do you want go out in the playground?" she asked.

"That would be nice." I was glad of the distraction as Wendy and I chatted to her friends and I began to feel a bit brighter.

That afternoon was history. Miss Penrose handed out work she wanted us to do, but as I looked down at my books my mind was in turmoil. I knew the only way I could deal with things was to forget about home when at school, and concentrate on my work instead. Keeping this firmly in mind, I picked up my pen and began writing.

I felt suddenly sick when Miss Penrose said it was time to go home. Tim's threats were on my mind. I was petrified but knew I had to keep it to myself and not let my feelings show.

Hazel, Maureen and I chatted on the bus and before long Hazel said, "Look, Christine; Tim's here."

I felt ill as she mentioned his name but did my best not to show it. A little voice inside my head was screaming that I didn't want to see him, but I behaved as normally as I could.

Tim eyed me suspiciously as I got into the van. "Did you have a good day?" he asked.

I nodded. "Yes, everything's fine."

"Sam's waiting to see you. He's on morning shift this week."

I felt my mood lift and hoped Sam would help me with my homework.

When I got home, I went up to see Mum and offered to give her tea, keen to be as far away from Tim as possible. Sitting on the bed with her, I wished desperately that she was well, healthy and strong. These things would never have happened if she hadn't had a stroke. She wouldn't have allowed my brothers to have guns. Tim would not have had the opportunity to abuse me.

Later Sam helped me with my homework until I'd got the hang of it, then he and Tim went into the kitchen. I noticed they were speaking very quietly.

"I say we should concentrate on the Surrey stockbroker belt," I heard Tim say. "You have to admit, Sam, you've only got to look at those houses to know that they're wealthy."

I went out into the kitchen to get some water so I could wash before bed. Sam coughed and the pair fell silent.

"I want my water to wash then I'm off to bed," I told them.

"Just as well I put the kettle on," said Sam.

We waited until I had my water, and as I went upstairs I heard Sam say, "If that's the case we'll need a pair of binoculars."

I said goodnight to Mum, washed and went to bed.

Once again, I was up and dressed before Tim could call me. "When Sam finishes work later he's going to help me make some rings," he said as he dropped me at the bus stop. "I'll take you with me on Saturday when I go to sell them."

I didn't want to go but knew I had no choice.

"No need to look so glum," he said, and I could feel he was smiling at my displeasure.

As I got on the bus and chatted to my friends, I felt the tension start to drain away. It was a good day and Wendy and I had fun choosing material to make knickers in sewing class. The idea made us giggle all afternoon.

That evening Sam was admiring some of the rings Tim had made when I came down after giving Mum her tea. "They look as good as the ones for sale in the jewellers," he said.

"That's the plan. If they look good enough I should be able to pass the zircons off as diamonds," chuckled Tim.

"Of course they look good enough. I can't get over the way they sparkle." Sam held a ring up to the light. "What do you think, Christine?"

"Beautiful," I told him. "I love the way it sparkles in the light."

"I'm sure you'll make a good profit, Tim," said Sam, patting him on the back.

"I hope so. I've told Christine I'll buy her a coat."

I was keen to get away and went upstairs to see Mum. I told her about the rings Tim was making and how I was making a pair of knickers in sewing class, which amused her. I found Radio Luxembourg and lay down besides her listening to the music. I relaxed so much I fell asleep, and Sam had to wake me and send me to my own bed.

Chapter Eighteen

SATURDAY ARRIVED. TIM and I were up early, quietly eating breakfast so as not to wake Dad as he slept after another night shift. I hated having to go with him. My father had handed my care over to Tim, allowing him total control over me and making him think of me as his property. He must have thought he could trust Tim to look after me, but it left me vulnerable and dependent on him, something that should never have happened.

Tim collected his rings and we got in the van. "I know a few people who'll be interested in buying diamond rings," he said. "I expect you to keep your mouth shut and leave the selling to me."

"I will," I said. I wanted nothing to do with selling them.

We headed for Falmouth first, with Tim reminding me that if we had a good day he was going to buy me a coat. I didn't like the thought of being beholden to him. As we joined the main road, he started to drive faster. I felt nervous and clung to my seat. "What's up with you?" he asked.

"I'm just worried about having an accident like we did with

Roy."

Tim laughed. "That was his fault, silly old git."

I was too scared to argue and continued clinging to my seat until we reached Falmouth. Tim looked at me as if I were pathetic. "Well, we've managed to get here without having an accident," he said.

I thought it was more luck than judgement, but was too afraid to say anything. We found somewhere to park near a shop Tim wanted to visit, and he reminded me again to keep quiet. I had to run to catch up with him as he picked up his bag and began striding off.

"We should do all right in here," he said, peering into the shop window.

I held back as he opened the door. "Come on in then," he said when he saw I was reluctant. I followed him inside.

"Oh," said the woman behind the counter. "I was thinking I haven't seen you for ages."

"I've been busy," said Tim. "I've got diamond rings for you. Just wait until you see them."

The woman's eyes lit up as Tim let her look in his bag. "Gold rings with three diamonds in a platinum setting," he told her proudly.

Once she'd taken them out of the box I could see she was smitten. "I'll let you have them on the cheap," said Tim.

She looked at me. "Doesn't your Daddy make beautiful rings, dear?"

I felt awkward. "Yes," I replied.

She looked sorry for me and turned back to Tim. "You're sure they're diamonds, aren't you?"

"Yes absolutely certain."

"You wouldn't see me off now, would you?"

"No of course not," he assured her.

"I'm sorry I had to ask," she said. "But I've been seen off before."

Tim looked disgusted. "That's dreadful. Some people have no shame."

The two of them began to discuss prices. I knew Tim wouldn't want me to listen, so I moved away but could still hear quite a bit of haggling going on before they reached an agreement, and the woman bought two rings and a few brooches. Tim stuffed the cash into his wallet and could barely contain his delight when we got outside. "Didn't I tell you she'd be a soft touch?"

"Yes."

"We'll go to this old bloke next," he said, looking at his list. "We should be able to get a few bob out of him. He's loaded. You'll be able to have a new coat, so you should be delighted."

He stared at me, waiting for my reaction.

"I am," I said.

He nodded.

Tim managed to persuade the next man that he was selling genuine diamonds and once again stuffed a wad of cash into his wallet. The shop had been dark and creepy and I was glad to get out of there. As promised, Tim took me to buy a navy-blue gabardine raincoat. It was lovely and I thanked him. He was in a great mood and suggested we get some groceries on the way home. I didn't want Mum to be left out and asked if we could get her some grapes.

We drove home eating iced buns we'd bought as Tim wondered aloud if Sam had bought the binoculars he needed. I was puzzled as to why he'd need them but thought little of it. I began feeling happier, thinking the day hadn't been so bad. I couldn't wait to give Mum her grapes and show her my coat.

That evening Sam came home and told Tim he'd got the binoculars at a shop in Plymouth. I was intrigued, and when they said they were going up to my bedroom to look out of the window, I followed behind along with Dad.

"Just look at the magnification," said Sam. "You can see the clay works up real close. Take a look, Tim."

He took the binoculars. "It's unbelievable how much bigger everything looks," he said, sounding amazed and handing them to me.

"Gosh!" I said. "It brings the clay works up close; you'd think they were right outside our house!"

Sam and Tim laughed.

"Let's have a look then," said Dad. Tim handed them over. "They must have been expensive," said Dad as he scanned the landscape.

"Yes, I have to admit they were expensive, old man," said Sam.

"But they'll pay for themselves," added Tim. Dad looked bewildered.

After tea, Dad went upstairs to sit with Mum and as soon as he was out of hearing my brothers began talking about finding a property to break in to. I kept quiet, knowing I'd get in trouble if I spoke.

"It only means pulling off the right job and we'll be made for life," Sam told Tim. "We'll have to watch a house for a while to see when the place will be empty."

I got fed up of listening and went upstairs to be with my parents. Sam eventually popped his head round the door and said he was going to the pub. When he'd gone, Dad said to Mum with a grin, "Sam likes his Saturday nights out, doesn't he? Do you remember the night he came in and promised to buy me some little cows and little sheep?"

Mum smiled. "I can't help wondering how many drinks he'd had then."

I giggled. "That's funny," I said.

"Yes, but he wouldn't admit saying it the next day once he was sober," said Dad. "So I never got my little cows or little sheep, did I, Ruby?" Mum smiled and shook her head.

"That's the way of it," said Dad. "It was a nice thought all the same."

* * *

Sam and Tim were keen to get out the following morning and use their binoculars. Tim asked if I wanted to go, but I needed to wash my school clothes and was glad to have that as an excuse. I asked Dad to wash my hair so that Tim didn't have to do it.

When my brothers came home they walked into the kitchen where I was emptying the bowl. They were so engrossed in conversation, they didn't notice me. Before they saw I was there

I'd heard enough to know they were talking about breaking in somewhere. I tried not to think about it as I went to sleep that night.

Tim was waiting for me after school the next day. "Sam's working late so you're going to have to help me," he said.

"Help you with what?"

"Help me with making the rings, of course." He sounded annoyed.

"I'm not sure I can."

"I've got it all set up at home. Once we get in we'll get on with it."

I realised he wasn't going to let me get out of it.

"You saw Sam doing it the other day, so you know what to do," he said, handing me the bellows. As soon as I caught hold of them I realised they were heavy. "Start pumping then," he said. I did my best but it wasn't long before they became too heavy for me.

"I can't do it anymore, Tim."

He looked furious. "Don't stop now, you stupid little fool," he screeched. "You can see the metal's just started melting."

Tears filled my eyes, but I knew better than to disobey. "It's too hard for me," I begged. I felt a searing pain on the side of my head as Tim clouted me.

"I need to melt the gold to make rings to sell," he yelled.

"It's not my fault I'm not strong enough," I wept, my arms in agony.

"I bought you a raincoat didn't I, you silly little sod? Where do you think the money came from?"

I flinched at the reminder. Tim carried on. "If it was left to the old man you would be getting soaking wet every day. You should be bloody well grateful."

I knew Tim would never let me forget the raincoat. I pumped the bellows as fast as I could. The pain in my arms was unbearable and the heat of the fire burned my face. Sweat ran down my cheek, my throat was dry, and my ear was throbbing from where Tim had hit me. I felt sick, but the fear of what would happen if I dared to stop pushed me on.

"Right, you can stop now, the fire's hot enough," he said eventually. I fell to the floor and watched as he took the pot from the flames and poured the bubbling gold into the moulds. "What was all the fuss about?" he asked, looking at me in disgust.

I was too frightened to reply. I struggled to my feet and went to the kitchen to get a drink. Dad had drawn water from our well that morning and its coolness was refreshing. As I began to relax, the familiar bang came from above of Mum's walking stick. Tim spoke sharply. "Mum needs the bedpan. Go upstairs and see to her."

"My arms are too tired to lift her," I said.

"Stop moaning. I do it all day when you're at school. Get up there."

As I climbed the stairs I wished for the millionth time that Mum had not had a stroke.

"I need the bedpan, Christine," she said. She looked frail, her skin a ghostly white. My heart went out to her.

"I'll try," I said, picking up the bedpan and lifting the sheets.

"I'm sorry I can't help you, dear." Her speech was slurred.

"I'm completely useless."

"It's not your fault, Mum," I said, doing my best to lift her without hurting her.

"It's too hard for you," she said, "call Tim."

"I'm all right," I said, knowing how shouting for Tim would make him angry. I eventually managed to slide the pan under Mum's bottom. I listened as she weed and could tell she must have been dying to go.

She breathed a sigh of relief. "I've finished, Christine dear. You're a good girl. I'm glad I had you. You're much better than your brothers."

I wanted to cry. "I love you, Mum. I always will," I told her. I left the room to empty the bedpan and when I returned I climbed onto the bed for a cuddle.

"It won't be long before your father gets home," she said. I felt relieved. I stayed on the bed until I heard his motorbike arrive. He came into the house and had a few words with Tim before coming upstairs.

"How are my two favourite girls today?" he asked, smiling at us.

"We're okay," we said.

"Christine came up to give me the bedpan," said Mum.

"Thanks, Christine," he said. "Everyone has to lend a hand."

"Christine is a lovely girl and I'm so glad we had her," said Mum.

"I stopped at the village shop on the way home," said Dad. "I've bought some cans of vegetable soup for tea. I thought you'd like that, Christine?"

I was very hungry. "Yes please," I said. I knew my father was doing his best. I followed him downstairs to the kitchen, where Tim had already warmed himself some soup and was sat at the table eating.

"I managed to do some castings for the rings I'm making," he said to Dad. "Christine helped me pump the bellows."

"Jolly good," said Dad. "Nice little cottage industry you've got going on here. It wasn't too hard for Christine was it?"

Tim flashed me a threatening look. Knowing I would be alone with him again the next day, it wasn't safe to tell the truth. "No, I managed to do it," I said. Tim nodded at me. Dad passed me the soup and bread before preparing Mum's meal.

I ate in silence and escaped to my room as soon as I could. I hated being in the same room as Tim. As I went up stairs he called after me, thanking me for helping him. That was for Dad's benefit – to make it look as if I had pumped the bellows willingly. I said nothing. I went to my parents' room to say goodnight.

"You're not looking very happy," Dad said to me. "What's wrong?"

"Just an earache," I said. I didn't tell him who caused it.

"Perhaps you caught a draft in your ear," he said. "Keep it warm. It should be better in the morning."

"Yes," I replied. I kissed Mum goodnight and went to bed. My ear hurt and I cried quietly. Next morning I discovered wax on my pillow. I didn't feel well but I had to go to school because it was my only escape from Tim. I felt like running away but Tim had already threatened to find me if I did. I was glad to go to school but found myself spending a lot of the day worrying and wondering what I could do about my situation.

Wendy noticed I wasn't myself, so I told her about my ear. "You poor thing," she said. "Is it still hurting now?"

"No, the aching has stopped."

"If your ear starts aching again see the school nurse," she said, putting her arm around me.

"Thanks, Wendy, but I'm feeling better." She nodded. After we'd finished lunch we went outside and met up with Maureen and Hazel.

"How are you feeling now, Christine? Is your ear any better?" Hazel asked. I told her it was.

"That's good," said Maureen. "I couldn't help feeling sorry for you this morning."

We continued talking. I enjoyed having my friends around me and put the horrors of home to the back of my mind. I felt sorry when the bell rang because we were having a laugh. "Time to go in," sighed Wendy.

"See you on the bus," Maureen and Hazel called out to me.

We went back to the classroom and started getting on with our work. School became a haven, a place of safety where I could escape the ordeals I suffered at home. I always experienced a terrible sinking feeling in my stomach when it was time to go home.

Chapter Nineteen

I DREADED WEEKENDS, especially the weeks when Dad worked nightshift. I got really scared when I knew Sam was going out.

"Will you stay home tonight, Sam?" I asked one evening when Dad was on nightshift. I was hoping and praying he would say yes. I didn't want to be left alone with Tim again.

"I can't, Christine, I've made arrangements," he said impatiently.

"But please, Sam, couldn't you stay home just for once."

"I'm not stopping home just to please you, Christine," he snapped. "I look forward to my nights out, so forget it."

I was scared and upset. I wasn't used to Sam getting so angry. "What's up with her tonight?" he asked Tim.

"Don't take any notice. She's just in a funny mood this evening."

Sam put on his best aftershave – it turned out he was meeting a girl. As he went out and closed the door, a feeling of dread came over me. I felt sick and my stomach tightened. The sound of Sam's motorbike disappeared. I was trapped.

"I'm going up to see Mum," I said.

"No, you're not. You're going up and getting undressed. Go on, go upstairs and get undressed." He gave me a push. I felt sick as I climbed the stairs. I didn't want him looking at me and touching me. I was sure brothers weren't meant to do that. When I got to my room I kept my clothes on. I was determined I wouldn't let him touch me.

"Why haven't you got your clothes off?" he demanded.

"Please, Tim, don't make me get undressed. I hate what you're doing to me."

His eyes flashed with anger. "Fine," he said. "Then I'm going in to kill mother."

He stormed out and I raced after him, terrified of what he was going to do. Mum was asleep – she looked completely helpless. Tim picked up a pillow and placed it over her face and started suffocating her. I panicked and did my best to pull the pillow away as Mum woke up and began to struggle, panicking because she couldn't breathe. I was screaming for him to stop, tears streaming down my face as I tugged at the pillow. He held it down for what seemed like ages, his expression like a maniac's. Then he started to laugh, as if this was a game. Absolute panic must have given me strength because the pillow came apart at the seam.

As the feathers erupted into the room, Tim must have realised he'd gone far enough and removed the pillow. As Mum lay there gasping for air and trying to get over the shock, he began acting the clown. He picked up a clothes peg which was on the mantelpiece and put it on his nose. He made lots of silly faces and danced around the room in an attempt to make light of what had happened. He pretended what he had done had only been a joke.

"Go and get Mother a drink, Christine," he said. "She looks as if she needs one."

While I was gone Tim must somehow have managed to convince Mum he had been playing and wasn't really going to hurt her. She was gasping for breath while trying to laugh at him acting the clown. I suppose laughing could have been a nervous reaction on her part, some form of hysteria. I don't know what she was really thinking or feeling.

He took the beaker of tea from me and helped Mum to drink it. "Is that better, Mum?" he asked when she'd finished. She nodded. "Get the dustpan and brush, Christine, and clear away the feathers," he ordered. "We don't want to leave a mess for Dad."

I knew he wanted to cover his tracks so Dad wouldn't know what had happened. "Do you need the bedpan, Mum?" he asked nicely.

"Please, Tim," she said, still short of breath. She looked confused, but he seemed to have persuaded her it was all a bit of fun. He gave her the bedpan and then went to empty it.

"Are you all right, Mum?" I asked. She nodded and squeezed my hand. I was in shock myself with what had happened. Tim came back and put the bedpan under the bed.

"Say goodnight to your mother then," he told me.

"Goodnight, Mum," I said, bending down to give her a kiss.

"I'll look in and see if you're all right again later," said Tim. She smiled at him, unaware that what he'd done was to intimidate me into doing what he wanted. "It's time you went to bed as well, Christine," he said, as if nothing had happened.

He followed me into my room. "See what I mean?" he said, closing the door behind us. "It wouldn't take much for me to kill your mother. I'd just say she died in her sleep."

My mind was whirling. "The doctor would know," I said.

"No." His voice was cold. "She's been ill for so long they'd just sign the death certificate. Come on then, get undressed. There's been enough messing around this evening."

I felt helpless as he pulled my clothes off. I knew I didn't have any say in what was happening. I shuddered when his hands touched my skin. I hated him because of what he was doing to me and what he had done to Mum.

I stayed in bed late the following day as I didn't want to see Tim. He went out, and when I went in to see Mum and asked if she was okay, I got the feeling she didn't remember what had happened the previous evening.

Chapter Twenty

IT WASN'T LONG after this horrific episode that I started my periods. Mum and I were alone at home. It came as a real shock to me when I pulled down my pants in the toilet and found I'd been bleeding. I had no idea what was happening to me and ran to Mum in a panic. "I think I've hurt myself, Mum, I've got blood in my knickers." I said. "What's wrong with me?"

"It's all right, Christine, nothing to worry about," she said. "You've just started your periods, love. It's what happens to girls when they get older."

I felt I was about to faint and lay down on the bed beside her. "I should have told you before, but didn't expect you to start so early," she said, taking hold of my hand as I lay beside her. "You'll need sanitary towels, love. There's some in the bottom drawer of my wardrobe."

I went over and opened the wardrobe drawer to take a look. "Is this what you're talking about, Mum?" I asked, holding up a packet.

She nodded. "Yes, there should be a sanitary belt in there as well."

Mum explained what I had to do, how often my periods would come and said it was best to wash my knickers in cold water to get the blood out. She said she'd tell Dad so that I didn't have to.

"Does he need to know?" I asked feeling embarrassed.

"Yes, love. But it's all right. He'll understand." Her voice was just a whisper. She looked worn out and I could see it had been too much for her.

"All right, Mum, I'll leave it to you."

When I went up to see her later she reminded me about my knickers. I poured cold water into a plastic bowl and put them in to soak. I could see the water turning a brownish colour as the blood started coming out. Sam came in whistling a tune and saw what I was doing. "Christine's messed her pants!" he called out. "I've just caught her washing them."

I wanted the ground to open up and swallow me. Tim appeared. "Leave her alone, Sam," he told him. "You know very well what it is, don't tease her."

"Sorry," said Sam. I was too embarrassed to reply.

"Don't take any notice of him," Tim told me. I thought it odd that Tim was defending me. Sam made them both a cup of tea and they disappeared into the living room. I scrubbed my knickers with soap until they were clean and took them upstairs to put on a chair to dry.

Sleep was hard to come by in bed that night. I couldn't help wondering why no one had told me about periods. It would have prevented it from being such an ordeal. I must have fallen asleep eventually as Tim woke me up for school in the morning. "Are you feeling well enough to go?" he asked while I was eating breakfast.

"Yes, I'm fine," I said, not wanting to stay home with him. I was pleased to see Maureen and Hazel waiting at the bus stop, and once we were on the bus I told them I'd started my periods. We had a good chat and I changed my towel at lunchtime without any issues.

I felt a sense of foreboding as the school day drew to an end. Dad and Sam would be at work when I got home and I didn't know what mood Tim would be in. I wondered if he would be making rings and force me to pump the bellows, or worse, make me take my clothes off and touch me. What could I do about it? I wanted to run away but felt too afraid to leave my mother. I knew how upset she'd be if I didn't come home from school that evening. And I had no money and nowhere to go. I kept up the pretence that nothing was wrong until I got home, and was relieved beyond belief to see Mrs Hendy had come to visit and was upstairs with Mum.

"Hello, my little dear," she said, giving me a hug. "I hear you're getting on well at school."

"Yes, I like it there. I've made lots of new friends," I told her.

"That's good, dear. I'm glad. I've brought an apple and blackberry pie for you all to enjoy."

Tim brought the three of us a cup of tea and I helped Mum with hers as Mrs Hendy chatted away. Tim called me downstairs for tea, and I went immediately as I knew he'd be angry if I didn't do as he wanted. Jim Hendy soon arrived to collect his mother and I popped upstairs to see if I could help carry her bag.

"I can hang on to the stair rail better if my hands are free," she said. "It's this blooming arthritis, you see."

Sam came home soon after Mrs Hendy and Jim left, and it seemed I'd escaped from Tim for another evening.

The following afternoon, Friday, Tim reminded me he wanted me to attend an auction with him the next day. "Don't forget," he said, as he drove me home from the bus stop. "If you've got homework, you'd better do it tonight."

"All right" I replied reluctantly.

"It'll be fun. I'm hoping to bid on some nice pieces of jewellery," he said. "You can choose a piece for yourself if you want to."

"Perhaps," I replied.

He seemed to be getting wound up. "I've gone and lost the minute hand from the watch I'm repairing. I need you to find it for me when we get home."

"I'll try," I said.

"You'd better. I said I'd have it repaired by tomorrow."

I was really worried and as soon as we got home I was on my hands and knees under the table. "Is the minute hand black?" I asked.

"Of course it is, stupid. That's what makes it so hard to find. Hurry up."

Within a few seconds he asked if I could see it. "Not at the moment," I replied.

"Well, you'd better stay there until you do," he snarled.

I knew my life wouldn't be worth living if I didn't find it and began running my hands along the floor. I was so relieved when I managed to find something, but it was only a screw.

"Keep looking until you find it," said Tim.

I ran my hands over a larger area and my fingers came into contact with something else. "I think I might have found it," I said, coming out from under the table.

"That's it," said Tim. "I'll be able to finish this job now and then get tea."

Just as he finished speaking, Mum knocked on the floor above. "Go up and see to her, Christine," he said. "You can see I've got a lot to do."

"I was going up to see her anyway," I said.

After seeing to Mum, I told her Wendy had invited me to the cinema again and wanted me to stay over at her house. "Do you think I'd be allowed to go?" I asked.

"Ask Tim," she said. "If he agrees perhaps he'll take you into town to meet her."

I felt crushed. I always had to ask Tim's permission to do anything. I don't know why Dad allowed this to happen.

"I'll ask him later," I said. "He's still busy at the moment."

"I'll have a word with him too," said Mum.

* * *

Tim drove like a crazy man toward Wadebridge and seemed to enjoy scaring me. He lost out on the first lot he bid on at the auction, but his mood lifted as the day progressed and he had more success. He bought a bracelet I selected, and I made up my mind to ask him on the way home about the cinema and staying at Wendy's. I could see he didn't look very pleased about it.

"I'll drop you in on the Saturday morning, but I don't want you staying at her house overnight the night before," he said. "It's not as if we know them at all, so I really can't allow that."

Tim had total control over my life. He ruled me and dominated me, and deep down I'd known all along he wouldn't want me to stay over – he didn't want to let me out of his sight. But I was just pleased that I'd be going to the cinema.

As we drove along we saw a couple at the side of the road. "Hitchhikers," said Tim. "I'll give them a lift."

I was surprised he was being so nice to complete strangers as he pulled over and the couple ran up to the van.

A young blonde man came to the window. "Could you give us a lift, please?" he said.

"Yes, sure," said Tim. "Where are you heading?"

"Bodmin. Are you going near there?"

Tim nodded. "Yes, as long as you don't mind riding in the back."

"Thank you. It's only me and my girlfriend."

Tim and the young couple chatted as we drove along. They were over from France and wanted to practice their English.

"Do you know anywhere cheap where we can stay overnight?" the man asked as we pulled over to let them out.

"Yes," said Tim, getting out the van to open the back door for them. "That's a good place over there." He pointed across the road towards a large building.

"Is it cheap?" the man asked.

"Yes, it's cheap, and I'm told they do a good breakfast."

I stared to where Tim was pointing, and it was the gates of St Lawrence's Hospital, the psychiatric unit in Bodmin.

"Ah, thank you, we are really grateful," said the man. "We'll see if they have vacancies."

As the couple walked away waving and smiling, I stared at Tim in shock. What in the world was wrong with him? "What are you doing sending them into the mental hospital?" I said.

He roared with laughter, and again I saw something maniacal in his eyes. "They asked for cheap bed and breakfast, didn't they?" he said. "They'll soon find out and anyway, they should be bloody grateful for the lift."

I didn't say anything else, but his cruelty shocked me. Who was he doing that for? What did he get out of it? When we got home I told Sam about the hitchhikers and was sad that he found it amusing too. He could see that I didn't approve.

"Christine doesn't seem too pleased about that," said Sam, still laughing.

"No, but she liked it at the auction," said Tim. "Just look at the lots I bought." He put them on the table. "That's the bracelet Christine likes. I said she can have it."

"Try the bracelet on, Christine," said Sam, handing it over.

"I love it and it fits perfectly," I said, holding it up for them to see.

"It looks really nice on you," said Sam. "Perhaps you can wear it to the school Christmas party."

I looked over at Tim. "Yes, you can wear it if you want," he said.

"Can I? I've never worn anything as nice as this."

"Take care of it, mind. And make sure you don't lose it."

"I promise I won't."

"So, is he forgiven for sending those frogs into the mad house?" asked Sam.

"Yes, but it wasn't a very nice thing to do," I said.

"They'll be all right; don't worry about a couple of frogs," said Sam.

"I expect they were hopping mad when they found out!" said Tim, and they both laughed.

"I'm going up to see Mum and show her my bracelet," I said, feeling disgusted.

Chapter Twenty-One

THE FOLLOWING MONDAY at school, Wendy was delighted that I was able to go to the cinema with her that weekend and hoped I'd be able to stay over another time. I doubted it.

Mrs Wilson revealed the school was planning a Christmas dance instead of the usual party. We were all very excited and I was so pleased when she said the whole year was invited, meaning Maureen and Hazel would be able to go.

"Can we have pop music, Miss?" someone called out.

"Could we have music like on Six-Five Special?" another asked.

Mrs Wilson smiled. "If that's what you want I'm sure we can arrange it."

"Isn't it exciting," Wendy said to me lunchtime. "It will be nice having a dance instead of the usual Christmas party."

"Yes, it sounds wonderful. I hope I'll be allowed to come."

"Why wouldn't you be?" Wendy looked puzzled.

"Because it's being held after school," I said. "I don't know if

Tim will bring me."

"Can't you come in on the bus with Maureen and Hazel?" asked Wendy.

"Maybe, but only if Tim lets me."

She looked concerned. "Well, I hope so. Why don't you ask him over the weekend?"

"I'll try, but it was hard enough persuading him to let me go to the cinema."

"I could ask him for you, when he drops you off? Would you like me to do that?"

I bit my lip. I knew Tim was fine about me going to a party during school hours, but now it was an evening dance it was a different matter. "You can if you like," I said. "I just hope he doesn't get angry."

"Don't worry, leave him to me," she said, patting me on the shoulder.

Outside after lunch we soon spotted Maureen and Hazel. "Come on, let's go over and see what they've got to say," said Wendy, grabbing my arm. "Have you both heard about us having a Christmas dance?" she asked as we approached them.

"It's exciting isn't it?" said Hazel, her eyes lighting up.

"So exciting," said Maureen.

"I've never been to a dance before, I hope I'll be allowed to go," I said.

"Of course you will, Christine," Wendy assured me. "I'll make sure Tim agrees."

"You could catch the bus in with us," said Hazel, putting her arm around me.

"Maybe, I'll have to wait and see." I didn't want to get my hopes up.

"Stop worrying, Christine, I'll persuade him," said Wendy. I smiled at her.

"And if he doesn't agree when Wendy asks, we'll ask him as well," said Maureen. Hazel nodded, and I was so glad to have such good friends.

On the bus home, Hazel and Maureen discussed what they might wear to the dance. They had great outfits planned. I didn't know if I'd be going, and even if I were allowed to go I felt I had nothing to wear. The girls said I looked great in my tartan trews and that I could wear those.

When I got home, Mum said Aunty Mary had visited and left some pasties for us all. She had also left a present for me. "It's on that chair," said Mum, pointing to a bag. "She says she hopes you like it."

I picked up the bag and couldn't open it fast enough. The first thing I saw was a lovely pink sweater. "What a beautiful sweater!" said Mum. "It's your favourite colour too"

"Yes! And a black polka-dot skirt as well as bobby-dazzler socks!" I squealed in excitement. "They're the latest fashion, Mum. How kind of Aunty Mary."

She smiled, glad to see me happy. "Try them on for size," she said. "Aunty Mary will take them back and change them if they're not right."

I didn't have to be told twice. I put the clothes on and twirled in front of the mirror, feeling a million dollars. They fitted beautifully, and the skirt was the right length too.

"You look lovely, Christine," said Mum. "You'd better put them in your wardrobe. You can wear them to your school party."

Downstairs Sam asked what Aunty Mary had left for me. He was surprised when I told him. "Gosh, she's spoiling you, giving you all that. I hadn't expected you to get anything seeing as Tim knocked Roy off his bike."

I'd feared the worse after that crash, but Roy must have made light of it and laughed it off. I was relieved Aunty Mary was still fond of me and didn't think badly of us.

* * *

Saturday morning soon arrived, and Tim was waiting to take me to the cinema. He was surprised I wasn't wearing my new clothes.

"I'd rather keep them until the school party," I said. I still hadn't told him how plans had changed, and it was now being held in the evening.

"You'll look really nice and you can wear your new bracelet," he said. "Your friends will be amazed at how lovely you're looking."

I blushed and felt awkward as he glanced across at me. "Don't forget make sure you're waiting for me once the cinema's over."

"I will be," I assured him.

"Good, because I need you to help me choose a Christmas present for Mum. I thought we could take a look around the shops together."

"I'd like that," I said. "We'll try to find something special for her."

Wendy saw us pull up outside the cinema and came walking towards us. I felt pleased as she smiled at Tim and he smiled back. "So, you're Christine's friend Wendy," he said, winding down his window.

"Yes, thanks for bringing Christine in to go to the cinema."

"That's all right. We're going to buy a few Christmas presents after."

"That'll be nice," said Wendy. I could see she was winning him over. "Anyway, now you're here Tim," she said. "I was hoping to ask you a favour."

He looked surprised. "What's that then?"

"Well, it's about our school party. We've been told that instead of it being in the afternoon it'll be in the evening."

"Why's that?" said Tim.

"Mrs Wilson said it's more suitable now we're getting older," said Wendy. "So could you bring Christine along and also Maureen and Hazel?"

Tim turned to look at me and I found the courage to speak. "Would you, Tim, please," I asked. "It would save them catching the bus?"

"If that's what you want," he said. I breathed a huge sigh of relief.

"Thanks, Tim," said Wendy. "Come on, Christine. We'd better join the queue. They're starting to go in. See you later, Tim."

I got out of the van and was relieved when Tim drove away. I grinned at Wendy. "See!" she said. "I told you I'd persuade him, didn't I?"

"Thanks, Wendy. I didn't think you would."

"Well, you can stop worrying about it now."

We went in and watched a Popeye cartoon, with everyone singing along to the theme tune. Then we watched a Tarzan film. I was delighted with the whole thing. I'd been to the cinema a few times with my parents, but this was the first time I'd been with a friend. Wendy even treated me to an ice cream at the interval, and I was sorry to see the final curtain when the film was over.

"I really enjoyed it; I just wish it lasted longer," I told Wendy. She smiled and looked pleased.

"You'll have to come along with me again," she said, giving me a hug.

The light seemed very bright when we got outside. Tim was already there waiting for me and Wendy told us to enjoy our Christmas shopping.

The shops looked beautiful all decorated for Christmas. Tim looked in the windows of some of the jewellery shops, wanting to compare the rings on display to the ones he was making. "My rings look every bit as good, don't you think?"

"Yes," I replied, not convinced but too scared to say otherwise.

We bought Mum two bed jackets. This was my idea and I selected a pink one and blue one to match her pretty flowery nightdresses. Tim said Sam had given him some money to buy me a Christmas present. I thought that was really kind and I told Tim I'd like some new shoes. I wanted a pair to go with the outfit

Aunty Mary had bought me, and chose some black patent ones with little kitten heels and a strap across the front that was all the fashion. I felt real pride in owning my first pair of high heel shoes – I was over the moon.

"Thanks, Tim," I said.

He nodded. "That's all right, but don't forget to say a big thank you to Sam when you get home."

"I will," I said as I danced out of the shop.

"The fruit shop next," said Tim. "Dad wants me to get mother some grapes."

I followed in anticipation, keen to choose her the best ones I could. "You get the grapes and I'll sort out the rest," he said.

I spent some time choosing the nicest grapes I could, before Tim returned with a basket full of fruit. "A treat for us at Christmas," he said, smiling to see the look on my face. "I got apples, pears, a pineapple, figs and dates." He was smiling like a Cheshire cat. I nodded.

"Could I interest you in a coconut, sir?" asked the shopkeeper when Tim was about to pay. "I'm selling them off, half price." Tim looked suddenly interested when he said half price.

"What do you think, Christine? Should I get one for Dad?"

"Yes, I'm sure he'd like that," I said.

"Do you know anything else he'd like?" he asked after we'd left the shop.

"He loves ginger beer," I replied without hesitation.

Tim nodded. "Why didn't I remember that?" he said, patting me on the shoulder. "Mother used to buy it for him every year. Where's the best place to buy that?"

"The Co-op," I said.

Once we had the ginger beer, we made our way back to the van and home.

"I can't wait to show Mum my new shoes," I said.

"Dad must be up by now," said Tim, looking at his watch. "He was still in bed when I left home because he's on nightshift tonight."

Panic gripped me. "I didn't know that. I thought he wasn't on nightshift until next week."

Tim was smiling. "He's changed shifts to help someone out. He's good like that."

The joy of my new shoes vanished. I was terrified as I realised I would be home alone with Tim. I showed Mum and Dad my shoes and told them how much I enjoyed the cinema.

"Have you got to go to work tonight, Dad? Can't someone else do it?" I asked.

"I'm sorry, love; no one else can do it and I can't let people down."

I felt like crying and must have looked upset. "It'll give me more time off at Christmas and that'll be good, won't it?" he said.

I remembered Tim's threats and violence towards our mother, so I tried to look happy. After Dad went to work, I sat with Mum then ate my tea. Tim made her a hot water bottle and snapped at me when I hesitated to take it up to her. I knew exactly what was going to happen once she was warm and sleeping.

I gave Mum the bottle and said goodnight. I was overwhelmed with despair as I went into my bedroom. I couldn't bring myself to take my clothes off so got in bed with them on. I pulled my blankets up over me as I heard Tim going into Mum's room. I was petrified and held my breath as he said goodnight before making his way to my room. I closed my eyes tightly hoping that if he thought I was asleep, he wouldn't bother me. I could hear him breathing heavily before he shook me.

"Don't pretend to be asleep," he said, pulling back my blankets. "Why didn't you get undressed?"

"I was feeling cold."

"Get undressed now, I'll soon warm you up," he said, before dragging me out of bed. A vision of him suffocating Mum flashed through my mind. I was helpless. I had to do as he said if I wanted to stop him from hurting Mum.

He tugged at my clothes. "Hurry up, we haven't got all night."

"I can do it," I said.

"I don't know why you're so bloody ungrateful," he snapped. "I took you to the cinema, didn't I? And let you choose new shoes."

"Yes," I replied. I took off my last item of clothing and got into bed.

"Don't pull up your blankets, I want to take a look," he ordered. I couldn't stop my tears from flowing and started to sob. "You can stop that right away," he hissed. "I'm only looking at you, what's all the fuss about?"

"I don't like it," I said.

"Don't be silly."

"Yes, but you're my brother, I don't think that it's right," I said between sobs.

"Shut up, there's nothing wrong with it!" he spat. I sobbed even harder as he prised my legs apart. "Stop your bloody crying."

I was terrified and tried to stop. "That's better," he said as I went quiet. I felt ill and went ridged as I felt him touching my private parts. I felt the bed shaking and could see he had started touching himself. "You should be doing this," he told me.

I could tell he was getting pleasure from humiliating me and felt repulsed by his actions. All of a sudden we heard Sam's motorbike and he jumped up. "That's Sam! What's he doing home already?" he said, zipping up his trousers before hurrying out of my room. I was so relieved to know Sam was back and Tim wouldn't be able to do anything else to hurt me.

"You're early," I heard Tim say.

"I thought I'd better get back; the roads are freezing up. I don't know how the old man's going to get home in the morning."

I heard Tim ask Sam if he wanted a cup of tea, as if nothing had happened.

I put my nightdress on and breathed a sigh of relief as I pulled the bedding up over me. I cuddled my hot water bottle but couldn't get to sleep. I felt tormented and wondered what to do, eventually falling asleep due to complete emotional exhaustion.

* * *

Sam could see something was wrong with me as he made me breakfast while Tim was outside putting snow chains on the van.

"Are you okay?" he asked.

"Yes, I'm fine," I lied, just as Tim came in.

Sam soon went upstairs, and Tim moved really close to me and said quietly, "Don't you dare mention what happened last night."

"I won't," I said. "I haven't."

"Keep it that way." He sounded evil. "Or I'll wipe the family out."

I pushed my plate aside, suddenly not hungry. "There's plenty of toast left for you," I said, wanting to shut him up. He just smiled.

Sam returned and they both began talking about Christmas. When Tim thought Sam couldn't see, he gave me a sinister stare that chilled me to the bone.

"Well, after the school dance tomorrow night you'll be breaking up for the school holidays," said Sam cheerfully.

My heart sank as he said it. I needed to be at school, out of the way, where I could forget about things. "Yes," I replied.

"It's all right, don't look sad," said Sam. "We'll make the best of it. We'll bring our mother downstairs on Christmas Day. You wait and see, it'll be just like old times."

"I hope so," I said. Tim glared at me across the table. "I'd better go up to my room and get everything sorted," I said.

Chapter Twenty-Two

IT WAS A lovely last day of term and when I got home to get ready for the dance, an overwhelming feeling of excitement came over me. I opened my wardrobe and still couldn't believe my luck having such beautiful clothes to wear. I found it hard to believe it was me when I looked at myself in the mirror. I was thrilled to see my skirt and sweater suited me so well and admired how well my black patent shoes went with my pink florescent socks.

"Isn't she looking lovely Ruby?" said Dad when I went into show Mum.

"She's beautiful," said Mum, beckoning me over. "I've got something for you, Christine."

"What is it?" I asked, as she passed me a little blue bottle.

"It's called Evening in Paris, love. Dab some behind your ears."

I took the small rubber stopper out and did as she said. "Doesn't she smell lovely, Jack?" said Mum.

"Yes, really nice, my dear," said Dad before giving her a kiss.

Mum and Dad couldn't say enough about how lovely I looked. It seemed to bring them so much happiness. It was as if a dark shadow entered the room when Tim came in.

"I've got your bracelet," he said, handing it to me. "Put it on."

"It's such a beautiful bracelet!" said Mum. "You look like a princess now, my dear. You'll be the belle of the ball."

I blushed.

"Even prettier with those rosy cheeks," chuckled Dad.

"Come on, then. Your friends will be waiting," said Tim.

I kissed my parents, went downstairs and out to the van.

"You're looking nice, I have to admit," said Tim. "Just make sure you don't have anything to do with any old boys."

Tim clearly thought I was his property. He'd told me on many occasions how he wanted us to live together as man and wife. It was dreadful.

"I won't," I told him. "I'll only be dancing with the girls."

"If I find out you have, you won't be allowed to go to anything else," he warned.

Much to my relief, we stopped to pick Maureen and Hazel up. I knew Tim wouldn't say anything else while they were in the van. He dropped us off and we arranged for him to collect us at 9.30pm.

"It's good of Tim running around after us," said Maureen when he'd gone.

"I think you're lucky, Christine, having such a nice brother," said Hazel.

I felt a strong impulse to tell them the truth, but knew it wasn't safe. I bit my tongue as we walked into the school hall and spotted Wendy.

"Wow! Look at her!" said Maureen. "I can't believe she's wearing lipstick; my mother wouldn't let me."

Hazel was impressed too. "She looks pretty," she said.

"You look beautiful, Wendy," I said when we'd crossed the room.

"So do you," she said. "You all look terrific."

We went to the cloakroom and Wendy asked if I'd like to try her lipstick. I hesitated. "It's pink and would look nice with your sweater," she said. "What's wrong, don't you like it?"

"It's not that. I'm afraid Tim will tell me off."

"Just take it off again before you leave," she said, passing it over.

Wendy offered her lipstick to Hazel and Maureen too. Maureen was worried what her mother would say but Wendy also persuaded her that she could take it off before she went home.

I put it on. "Aren't we all looking really grown up?" said Wendy proudly. "Well, come on then, the dance will be starting."

As we made our way down the corridor we heard music. "Come on, they're playing At the Hop!" shouted Wendy.

Maureen and Hazel started dancing as soon as we got there. "It's time to jive," said Wendy, grabbing my arm. I felt nervous and excited all at once as she pulled me onto the floor. I was glad Wendy knew what to do because I wasn't certain. "Wow! Wasn't that good?" she said when the music stopped.

"Fantastic!" I said.

"I love your bracelet, Christine," said Wendy. "I only realised you were wearing it when I saw it sparkle."

"It's the one we got at the auction," I said, but there wasn't time to say anything else because the music started up again and we began dancing to Peggy Sue.

"Could I have the next dance, Christine?" I heard someone ask. I turned around and saw Clive, who'd been in my junior class. I was going to accept until I remembered what Tim said.

"I'm sorry, Clive, I've promised to dance with Wendy," I said apologetically.

"That's all right, perhaps another time," he said. He was obviously disappointed.

Wendy looked puzzled. "You could have danced with him."

"I'd rather dance with you or one of the girls," I said.

"So you're not ready for a boyfriend yet?"

"No."

The dancing had made us thirsty, so we had some lemonade and ate some sausage rolls until Bird Dog started playing, "I love this one," squealed Wendy, dragging me onto the floor again.

I had a great time. "I thought you said you couldn't dance," laughed Wendy.

"I didn't think I could," I said as The Grand Coolie Dam began playing. "I love Lonnie Donegan. I can't stop singing along to this one when it's on the radio at home."

Wendy smiled. "I do exactly the same."

I enjoyed the rest of the evening and couldn't help laughing when Wendy started singing along to Good Golly, Miss Molly.

"This is going to have to be the last record," announced Mr Smith when Little Richard had stopped singing.

"Oh, No!" we all groaned.

"It's Kewpie Doll!" shouted Wendy. "I've been waiting for this one all evening."

"I don't want this night to end," I said.

"I know what you mean," she said. "Thankfully we've got Christmas to look forward to."

I felt a chill run through me at the thought of being around Tim so much. "I suppose so," I managed to say.

When the music stopped we ran to the toilets to take our lipstick off. Tim was waiting outside, and Maureen, Hazel and I jumped in the van.

"Happy Christmas," called Wendy, and we all shouted the same back to her. Tim asked if we'd had a nice time but was more interested to know if there had been any trouble.

Back at home I was happy to see Sam. "My goodness, don't you look posh," he said. "Where's my little sister gone, the one who made mud pies?"

"She's growing up, stupid?" said Tim.

"I can see that," said Sam.

I felt embarrassed to hear myself being discussed and felt awkward about growing up. "So, what was it like then? Did you enjoy yourself?" asked Sam.

I told him how much I'd enjoyed the night then went up to tell Mum and Dad all about it.

* * *

"I've got a job for you," announced Tim when I got up on Christmas Eve. I instantly feared he wanted me to pump the bellows again. "You can decorate the Christmas tree," he said. "We want it looking nice for when Mum comes down."

I was so relieved. "Yes, I'd like to do that," I said.

"Sam brought it home. It's in the back yard. Go on and eat your breakfast and I'll bring it in."

I ate my cornflakes and Tim started working on his jewellery. I was nervous of him but tried to make small talk. Mum soon needed me, so I went to help her with the bedpan and told her I was doing the tree. "Are the Christmas decorations still in the cupboard under the stairs?" I asked.

"I'm sure they are, in a cardboard box," she said.

I found the box, and wonderful memories of Christmas past came flooding out when I opened it. The box was too big for me to carry so I dragged it across the room before getting a chair so I could reach the top of the tree. I had such fun and was thrilled every time I found another decoration which I'd forgotten. I put the star on top and stood back to admire my work.

"You've done a good job," said Tim.

"Do you think Mum will like it?" I asked.

"Yes, of course she will, it'll make her Christmas."

That evening Dad asked if I'd like to help him in the kitchen. I wanted to make the day go faster so I peeled the sprouts.

"You'd better go to bed early," Sam told me as he was getting ready to go out. "Santa won't come to you unless you're fast asleep."

"Stop being so silly, Sam. I'm too old to believe that," I told him.

He pretended to be surprised. "Are you?" It doesn't seem

long ago that you did."

"I haven't believed in Father Christmas for ages," I said, and he started laughing.

I slept soundly knowing that even though Sam had gone out, my father was in the house. Next morning I was excited to find a pillowcase full of presents at the bottom of my bed. I was opening my gifts when Dad popped his head round the door.

"You found your presents then?"

"I've got nail polish and a manicure set from Aunty Alice," I said. "And look Dad isn't this stationery set pretty? Victoria sent me that."

"It's lovely, my dear."

"I love the books you and Mum got me. I'll be reading them for hours."

"I thought you'd like those. Right, I'm off downstairs to sort the turkey."

"I'll be down in a while, Dad. I haven't opened everything yet."

"Take your time, love. There's no rush."

Sam looked in next. "What a lazybones, laying in bed on Christmas Day."

"I'm getting up now. I've been looking at my new books."

"What new books have you got?"

"I've got Heidi. I've already started reading it."

"And Treasure Island and the Railway Children as well?" he said.

"I know," I told him. "Aren't I lucky?"

He laughed. "Yes you are, that'll keep you busy. Anyway,

you'd better get up we'll be taking Mother down soon."

I was keen to see Mum come downstairs so I got up right away. I got a blanket for her easy chair next to the Cornish range in the living room where she always used to sit, so that she could be as cosy as she liked when Sam and Dad carried her down.

"The dinner's ready. Could you bring out the plates?" Dad asked me.

"It smells good," said Sam as I carried the plates out to the kitchen.

"You've made a good job of the turkey, old man," said Tim as we sat to eat at the farmhouse table in the living room.

"I'll have mine and give Mum hers later," said Dad quietly. "It's a bit too hot for her at the moment and I'll have to mash it up."

"Mum can only manage it bit at a time otherwise she chokes, doesn't she?" I asked.

"Yes unfortunately, love."

"Mum's enjoying it by the fire," I said as I looked over to her.

"Yes, she's looking happy enough," agreed Sam.

Mum didn't seem quite with it, if truth be told, as she sat there in silence.

After we'd all finished eating, Dad began giving Mum her food. Sam told him it was the best meal he'd had in ages and roped me in to do the washing up.

"It was lovely, I'm full up for the first time in ages Dad," I told him.

"Come over and sit by your Mum," said Dad after we'd finished with the dishes. "I think I ought to chop a few logs, we seem to be running out."

"All right, Dad. I'll look after her," I said, and after he'd gone I turned to my mother. "Do you like the tree, Mum?"

She didn't seem to hear me and kept staring into the fire instead. "What are you doing, Mum?" I asked as she started picking at her blanket.

"I'm picking fresh grass, dear," she said. I thought what she said was funny and started laughing.

"There's no grass here, Mum," I said, thinking it was a joke.

"Stop laughing, you stupid fool," snapped Tim. "Haven't you got the sense to see that something's wrong?"

I don't think any of us had realised she was as poorly as she was, and her sudden deterioration came as a shock. "What do you think is wrong with her, boy?" Tim whispered to Sam.

"I don't know," he said quietly. "It could be a blood clot passing over the brain. It's worrying whatever it is."

Tears welled up in my eyes. I didn't want to believe what they were saying and moved myself closer to her just in time to stop her from putting her fingers in the fire. "What are you doing, Mum?" I asked.

"I'm stoking the fire, love," she said.

I was in a panic now. "But you're not using the poker, Mum," I said. "Don't put your fingers near the fire. You'll end up burning yourself."

"Run out and fetch father, Christine. Tell him it's urgent," said Sam.

Both of my brothers stood above her, looking alarmed. "Tell him not to hang around," shouted Tim as I darted towards the door.

I ran into the garden. "Dad you're needed, Mum's not right. She's acting strange."

He dropped his axe and ran indoors. "What's wrong?" he asked Sam and Tim. We explained about her picking the blanket and trying to poke the fire with her fingers. Dad knelt beside her. "How are you, Ruby?" he asked gently.

He looked so worried when she didn't respond, merely picking at the blanket covering her knees. "I'll get the doctor if she's no better in a few days," he told us.

"I'll sit here and look after her," I said as Dad went out to get the logs.

"Perhaps we should take her back up to bed," Sam whispered to Tim. "It doesn't seem to have done her any good bringing her downstairs."

"Wait until the old man comes back in, see what he has to say," Tim whispered back.

I put my arm around Mum to protect her as much as I could. I'd been so looking forward to having her downstairs with us for the day and didn't want her to have to go back up to bed.

Dad returned with the logs and the three of them agreed to take Mum up to bed where she could have peace and quiet. My heart sank.

"It's for the best, love," said Dad, noticing the anguish on my face.

I watched with a lump in my throat as she was carried upstairs. "She'll be all right when she's had a rest," said Sam winking at me.

I hoped he was right.

My father and brothers tried to make light of the situation for the rest of the day. We ate turkey sandwiches followed by figs for tea. I tried the pineapple too. Dad went upstairs to be with Mum and said I could go up for a little while but not to tire her. She didn't respond to me when I spoke to her.

"I'm so worried, Dad," I said.

"We'll just have to wait and see, love," he said. "I'm sorry Christmas hasn't turned out how you wanted it to."

I didn't want to go back downstairs so went straight to my room. The situation was obviously serious and I was devastated. As soon as I closed my bedroom door I collapsed onto my bed and burst into tears. I cried for ages, soaking my pillow through. I had been hoping for a nice Christmas with Mum, but it had ended up being the worst Christmas yet. I tossed and turned for what seemed like an age before drifting off to sleep.

Chapter Twenty-Three

MY MOTHER WAS the only thing on my mind when I woke on Boxing Day. My heart sank when Dad said she was no better and that he and Tim were going to fetch the doctor. I went in to see her. "Dad's gone to get the doctor, Mum. You'll be all right," I said. She didn't respond.

Sam tried to reassure me until the doctor arrived. I waited anxiously while she examined her.

"What did she say, old man?" asked Sam after Dad saw the doctor out.

"That it is early days and we have to hope for the best," he said.

"Couldn't she give you any more details than that?" asked Tim.

"No."

Sam went to break the news to Aunty Alice and tell Dad's work he'd need a few days of annual leave. Dad went upstairs to Mum and I began writing my Christmas thank you letters. I felt glad to have something to take my mind off what was happening and did my best to keep my writing neat.

"Victoria and Aunty Mary are going to be impressed," said Dad when I showed him my letters.

The minute Sam returned, Tim asked him if he'd asked Aunty Alice to make some pasties.

"Of course not, what do you think I am?" Sam chuckled.

"She'll be too worried about Ruby to bother with that," said Dad.

"That's you all over, Tim," said Sam.

"For goodness sake, don't make a fuss!" he said.

Dad quickly changed the subject and offered us all a fry-up. Sam offered to do it instead, and when we finished eating I said I was going to read my book.

"Which one are you reading now?" asked Sam.

"The Railway Children. I'm in the middle of it and I can't put it down."

"Go on then, love. You need a break from all this," said Dad. I felt relieved to get into my room, shut the door and lose myself in a book. Reading helped transport me from the dreadful realities of what was happening in my life.

After breakfast the following day I decided to tidy my bedroom. It kept me away from Tim and I wanted to show Aunty Alice I had a nice room. As soon as I heard the hinge on the gate creak, I ran down to greet her.

"How did you know I was here?" she asked.

"I listened out for you, I heard the gate creak."

"Gosh, you must have good ears," she said with a smile.

"How's your Mum? Is she any better?"

"Not really," I said sadly, watching Aunty Alice unpack freshly baked pasties. "You'll have to ask Dad. The doctor called earlier."

Tim walked into the kitchen. "Thanks, Aunty Alice. I was hoping you'd bring pasties."

"I had to," said Aunty Alice. "I didn't want to think of you all going hungry."

"Come on, let's go upstairs," I said, not wanting Tim to hold her up.

Dad was in with Mum and moved over so her sister could sit next to her. He explained to Alice that Mum was able to drink but hadn't spoken. Then he went quiet.

"It must all be very worrying for you," said Aunty Alice.

She offered to be any help she could, and Dad said that now I was older, I was able to help.

"Aunty Alice is here, Mum," I said, trying to get her to take notice. But she didn't stir, her eyes remaining closed

"Don't bother her, love. Let her rest," said Aunty Alice quietly.

"I've written two 'thank you' letters, Aunty Alice. Could you pass them on? One for Aunty Mary and one for Victoria"

"What lovely neat writing," she said after I'd handed them to her.

"Do you want to see my room as well?" I asked.

"Come on then," she said, getting up from the bed. I led her along the landing and into my room.

"Wonderful, you are keeping it nice. Not a speck of dust

anywhere," she said, running her finger over my dressing table.

"I cleaned it this morning," I said, feeling really chuffed.

"Well, it looks as if you learnt something while staying with me."

"I'm reading some nice books as well." I showed her the books I'd received for Christmas.

"That's good, I'm glad of that," she said.

We went back in to see Mum and Aunty Alice told Dad how well I'd done. "I'll go and make us a cup of tea," he said, before leaving us alone.

Aunty Alice caught hold of Mum's hand and gave her a kiss. "I hope she gets better soon, Christine," she said.

"Yes, I hope so too."

Tim joined us as Dad came up with the tea. "Did you have a nice Christmas, Aunty Alice?"

"Yes, not bad, Tim; fairly quiet, you know."

"I was hoping ours would be better," said Dad.

Aunty Alice looked sorry. "I'm visiting Victoria at Easter, Christine. Do you want to come with me? I'm sure you'd enjoy a break."

Tim butted in before I had chance to reply. "Christine won't be able to go with you, Aunty Alice. She's coming up to London with me."

Both Dad and Aunty Alice looked very surprised. I was in shock.

"To London you didn't mention it before?" said Dad.

"Why?" asked Aunty Alice.

"I'm going to Hatton Garden to get some more gems. I

thought it would be a good experience for Christine."

Aunty Alice looked disappointed. "Well, if that's what you want," she said turning to me. I must have looked horrified but she didn't seem to notice.

Tim was adamant. "It'll be nice for her. I can show her the sights."

"What about Mother?" asked Dad.

"Sam's having a few days off, he'll look after her."

"It sounds as if you've got it all worked out," said Dad. I desperately wanted to tell them that I'd prefer to go with Aunty Alice but felt too scared under Tim's steely glare.

"Perhaps you can come with me in the summer instead, love," she said.

"Yes, I'm sorry, Aunty Alice," was all I could manage to say.

Tim looked very pleased with himself as he got up and left the room. I had a lump in my throat and my eyes filled with tears. I turned away, not wanting Dad and Aunty Alice to see how upset I was. They carried on chatting until it was time for Aunty Alive to leave.

She gave me a hug. "I just want Mum to be all right again," I said quietly. "It isn't fair why her?"

"I don't know, love." She squeezed me tightly. "I wish I could tell you."

She kissed me and said, "Keep your chin up, I'm sure things will improve."

Later that evening Dad asked me to help with Mum's bedpan. As I made my way downstairs I could hear Sam and Tim talking in whispers.

"It's a powerful weapon" I heard Tim say. "I don't think anyone would argue with it, do you?"

"No not unless they're a complete idiot."

I crept along the passage hoping they wouldn't know I was there, but I stood on a loose floorboard.

"Did I hear a noise?" said Sam sharply.

"Yes, a floorboard," said Tim. I heard him coming up the stairs and froze to the spot. "Oh, it's you," he said. "Why are you creeping about?"

"I'm just emptying the bedpan for Dad."

Sam appeared behind Tim. "Don't get on to her, boy," he told Tim. "She's only helping our father."

"I suppose so," said Tim. "It's just she gave me a fright."

"I'm sorry, I didn't mean to," I said. "I'm off to bed now."

"Go on then, sleep tight," said Sam.

"See you in the morning," said Tim. As he turned away I noticed the gun in his hand. A chill ran through me as my suspicions were confirmed. I gave the bedpan back to Dad and wondered for a moment if I should tell him but I didn't dare.

* * *

"I'm off out tonight," announced Sam as we were eating breakfast on New Year's Eve. "I'd take you with me if you were old enough," he said, winking at me.

"What makes you think she'd want to go with you?" asked Tim.

"Why wouldn't she? You should go out more yourself."

"What bleeding business is it of yours?" snapped Tim,

AN INNOCENT GIRL

jumping to his feet and pulling a knife from his pocket. "I'm ready for a fight if you want one," he said, waving it at Sam.

My blood ran cold and I dropped my gaze to the floor. But Sam didn't seem at all frightened. "You've got no guts whatsoever, wanting to use a knife," he said. "If you were any sort of a man at all you'd use your fists."

I pushed my chair back and ran to the corner of the room as Tim took a swipe at Sam with the knife. "See what you've done, you're scaring your little sister," shouted Sam, grabbing at the blade.

Dad must have heard the commotion because he came running downstairs. He looked horrified to see Tim brandishing a knife. "What's going on here?"

"This idiot, father," said Sam. "He didn't like what I said and wants a fight."

"Come on, boys. Your mother's ill. This is the last thing she needs. If you care about your mother, Tim, put down the knife and call it quits."

"Do as he says, boy," said Sam. "We don't want to be responsible for making our mother any worse."

"For Mother's sake then," he muttered.

"Look at poor Christine. She's cowering in the corner," said Sam.

Tim looked at me. "All right, all right, forget about it now, it's all over."

Dad made a cup of tea for everyone and a hot chocolate for me in an attempt to cheer us up. "No more fighting," he said.

Chapter Twenty-Four

SAM AND TIM had no idea I was listening as they discussed ways in which they could get rich quick.

"I still say the stockbroker belt is worth looking at," said Tim.

"Maybe, but we've got to have it well planned."

"I'll size up a few houses on our return from London."

"I'm not sure about that; you'll have Christine with you."

"All the better. No one will expect anything if I've got a kid in tow," sniggered Tim.

"I suppose not," sighed Sam.

A feeling of dread came over me again at the thought of having to go with Tim to London. I went in to see my parents. Dad was pleased because Mum had managed to swallow some soup.

"I'll be going back to work soon," he told me.

"I'm sad you're going back," I said. I felt safe when Dad was home, but I couldn't tell him that.

"We wouldn't have any money to live on if I didn't, dear," he said. "Mrs Lane will look after your mother and you'll be back at school yourself next week." The thought of it cheered me up. "You could wash your uniform and get it all nice and ready," added Dad.

"Okay," I said, heading downstairs to get to work in the small metal tub in the kitchen. It wasn't long before my school clothes were hanging on the line and Dad came to see how well I'd done.

"Why didn't you tell me you were washing?" asked Tim coming outside. "I need a couple of shirts doing."

"Bring them down, Tim. I'll give Christine a hand to do them," said Dad.

"Could you do a few shirts for me?" asked Sam when he saw Tim with his.

"It's good drying weather, we might as well," said Dad.

I began scrubbing the shirt collars because they were quite dirty. "You're making a good job of that," said Dad.

Once I'd given the shirts a good wash I inspected them to make sure they were spotless. "I'll put them through the wringer for you," said Dad.

"You've got to mind the buttons, Dad," I said, standing next to him at the wringer. "I used to watch Mum do it and she was very careful with them."

Dad smiled. "You're a good girl. You'll make someone a lovely wife."

I blushed.

When we'd hung the shirts on the line we gave Mum a beaker of tea, but she didn't seem able to sit up. Dad explained that she was having problems with her balance. I gave Mum a kiss and went to read my book.

Dad soon came in to tell me it was raining and we should get the shirts in. I hurried down stairs, picked up the peg bag and ran out into the garden. The clothes were soon indoors and out of the rain.

"If you get the ironing board, I'll heat the iron up for you," said Dad. I was glad of his help. "I've wrapped a cloth around the handle so you don't burn yourself," he said. "I'll make the tea."

I wanted my school clothes to be perfect so began ironing them first, carefully putting each item on a hanger once I had finished.

"Make sure you do a good job of my shirt, I want it for Saturday night," said Sam. When I finished my uniform, I began ironing his clothing really carefully. I could feel the iron was getting cooler by the time I was ironing Tim's shirt, but I tried my best.

"You'll have to stop ironing now, I've got the tea ready," said Dad. I hung Tim's shirt on a hanger and put everything away. "You deserve this, love," said Dad, putting my tea on the table.

Sam and Tim joined us and started eating. "You've done very well today, Christine," said Dad, glancing at all the ironed clothes hanging up. "It's good of you to do your brothers' shirts."

"I don't think so," said Tim. "Why have you made a better job of ironing Sam's than you have of mine?"

"I couldn't help it, the iron started cooling down," I tried to explain.

"You think more of Sam than you do of me," he snapped.

"Leave her alone, you know that's not how it is," said Sam.

"Stop picking on her, Tim. She's done her best," said Dad.

"Well she's bloody useless. I'll have to do it myself." Tim glared at his shirt.

"That won't hurt you," said Dad. "Christine's done enough."

"But why is Sam's so much better then?" he asked. "She thinks a lot more of him than she does of me."

"Don't be so silly, son; you know that's not true."

I finished my tea as quickly as I could, desperate to get away. "I'm going to put my school clothes in my wardrobe, Dad," I said.

"Yes, you go on, love. Do what you have to do."

"Thanks for ironing my shirts for me," Sam called after me.

Dad popped into my bedroom to see if I wanted help washing my hair. "I doubt you want to ask Tim," he said.

I gratefully accepted. I wanted to have nice, clean hair to go back to school.

The next day Dad went to work and Mrs Lane came to help. As I helped her to turn and wash Mum, she mentioned that a district nurse would be coming twice a week. "They don't want you getting pressure sores do they, Ruby?" she said.

I thought Mum looked as if she knew what was being said but was unable to reply. "I think you know what I'm saying don't you, Ruby?" said Mrs Lane as we sat Mum up. I was thrilled to see her nod.

"I love you, Mum," I said, giving her a kiss on the cheek.

Tim was in a bad mood as he took me to catch the bus. When I told him I was looking forward to seeing my friends, he said he didn't know why I bothered and that I wouldn't see them when I left school. I didn't want to believe him.

It was lovely to see Maureen and Hazel again. Hazel wanted us to sniff her wrists as she had been given a cream perfume for Christmas. They were very sympathetic when I told them Mum had been so unwell. It was great to see Wendy too, and she reminded me that we'd agreed not to have school lunches any more. "We're going up to the fish-and-chip shop," she said. "And we can look round the shops after. I've brought some of my Christmas money. We can go to Woolworths."

I was really excited and the morning passed by slowly as I waited to go out with Wendy. I felt such a lovely sense of freedom when lunchtime came, and Wendy and I walked out of the school gates.

We both chose a fishcake and chips and Wendy said she'd pay if I grabbed a seat before the place got too full. "At least we're here before the others," she said, looking around. "There's a group from school who think they own the place."

The chippy soon got really busy and I was glad Wendy had known to get us here early. Once we'd eaten, we headed for Woolworths to get a fizzy drink before having a look round.

"What do you think of this lipstick?" asked Wendy.

"Yes, it looks really nice," I said. I marvelled at the beautiful nail varnishes on display. "I love this pearly pink one," I said, showing Wendy.

Wendy paid for her lipstick and we made our way back to school.

* * *

The week passed quickly and soon it was the weekend, which I'd been dreading because Sam would be going out and Dad was working nights. When Tim picked me up from the bus on Friday I didn't really want to speak to him so said I had a headache.

"Have a rest, you'll be having a late night tomorrow," he said. "Don't want you falling asleep on me."

I felt sick and rushed upstairs when I got home. But there was no escape from Tim, and the following evening, with Sam and Dad gone, I heard his footsteps on the stairs. I pretended to be engrossed in my book.

"Why aren't you ready for me?" He grabbed my book and threw it across the room. "You're wasting time. I expected you to get undressed."

I froze. "Well get your bloody clothes off then," he said, trying to rip them off.

"All right," I said, thinking of his attack on Mum, who was now even more vulnerable.

After he'd finished, he told me to stop whimpering. "You like it really," he said. "So stop pretending."

"I don't like it at all," I said. But he ignored me.

"I've been thinking about things," he said after a few minutes' silence. "If Mum dies, we could get a place together."

I was stunned. "I'll get a place where no one else knows us. It would be wonderful, Christine. We could live together as husband and wife."

I said nothing, but my insides were screaming that this was the last thing I wanted. "We'll talk about it another time," he said as he got up and left my room.

Back at school, I tried to forget the ordeal of the weekend.

Wendy and I invited Maureen and Hazel to the fish-and-chip shop with us. She suggested I could save the four of us a table while she placed our order in case the others didn't get there as early as us. Maureen and Hazel gave Wendy their money and the plan was made. We all enjoyed eating our lovely vinegary chips and fishcakes before making our way to Woolworths. As I gazed through the shop windows, I told myself to live for the moment.

Once inside, Hazel held up some knickers. "Look at these!" she said. "They're red and black!"

"They're nice! Really fancy," said Wendy.

"I wouldn't be allowed to wear them, they're see-through," said Maureen.

"You'll be able to wear what you like when you get older," Wendy told her. "Can we go to the shoe shop over the road now?"

"Of course," I said. "What do you need new shoes for, something special?"

Wendy grinned as we crossed the street. "Not really," she said. "I just like the new boy who works there."

"What new boy?" we chorused.

"Come inside, I expect you'll see him," said Wendy as we followed her in.

A good-looking boy quickly approached. "Am I able to help you?"

"Not at the moment thank you, we're only looking," said Wendy. I'd never seen her so coy. "I've seen a pair I like I'll come back on Saturday."

The boy gave her a smile. "I'll look forward to seeing you," he said.

Once we were outside and out of earshot, Wendy turned to us with a look of glee on her face. "He's gorgeous, isn't he?"

"Really nice I can see why you fancy him," said Hazel.

"I like his lovely wavy hair," I added.

"Are you really going back to buy those shoes?" asked Maureen.

"I might, if I can persuade Dad to give me the money."

"I can see you ending up with lots of shoes," giggled Hazel.

Chapter Twenty-Five

MUM WAS MAKING little or no progress as the spring term came to an end, with Mrs Lane coming in every day to take care of her. Tim was still talking about us living together. It seemed to be his fantasy, and I hated the idea and knew I needed to get away from him.

I was dreading our trip to London. My friends thought Hatton Garden sounded glamorous, but I didn't feel able to tell them why I was so against going. Wendy was heading to the seaside at Weymouth for Easter. I would have given anything to be going there instead.

Tim met me at the bus stop on the last day of term. "I've cleaned the van and filled up with petrol," he said. "Sam's home for the week so there's nothing to stop us." I didn't answer. "You're looking forward to it, aren't you?"

"Just worried about leaving Mum," I said.

"She'll be all right. She's got Dad, Sam and Mrs Lane taking care of her."

"Here she is, off to London tomorrow," said Dad when we got to Fir Tree.

Sam smiled and winked. "Off to the big smoke, hey?" I nodded. "You'll be all right with Tim," he said.

Dad added, "It's a big place, but Tim knows his way around."

"Make sure Christine sees the lights in Piccadilly, Tim," said Sam. "She'll love that."

"We'll see it all, don't you worry," said Tim, "Buckingham Palace and everything else too."

"You are a lucky girl, I wish I was going," said Dad.

I didn't know what to say other than, "I'll go up and change my clothes." I felt desperate and went in to see Mum. "I'm going up to London with Tim tomorrow, Mum." She looked vacant. "I'll bring you back a present." She blinked then. "I love you, Mum," I said, kissing her on the cheek.

That night I packed my clothes. I decided to wear my shorts and T-shirt under my clothes so I wouldn't need to get undressed for bed, feeling a bit safer as I laid them out for the morning. When I said goodnight to Dad he said he'd be gone by the time Tim and I left. "Have a nice time," he said.

Sadness overwhelmed me. I would have loved to have had the courage to tell my father I didn't want to go away with Tim, and why. I lay in bed stressing about it for a while before falling asleep with exhaustion.

The next thing I knew Tim was yanking the bedclothes off me. I leapt out of bed, my heart racing. He was in a rush to get going but I made sure I said goodbye to Mum and gave her a kiss. Sam gave me £3 for pocket money, which was a lot. I asked if he could afford it and he reassured me he could. Once I was in the van I fell asleep.

"Where are we now?' I asked when I woke up.

"We've passed Bristol and heading towards Swindon," said Tim.

"How much longer before we reach London?"

Tim looked irritated. "Nothing but questions from you since you woke up," he snapped. "We're making good time so bloody well shut up."

I didn't say anything else until we stopped for sandwiches, and Tim seemed to be in the mood to chat again. He showed me where he and Sam had lived on Gray's Inn Road in Central London. When we'd finished eating he said we'd be going over to Hatton Garden.

I was amazed at the beautiful shops and couldn't believe the prices of some of the jewellery. "They want £200,000 for this one," said Tim, showing me a diamond ring. "What do you think of that?"

"But that's a fortune. Who could afford it?"

"You'd be surprised, plenty of people."

"No one I know," I said.

We went into the shop where Tim used to work. He and the owner chatted away as we were led through various corridors towards the back of the building. Once we were tucked away, the man brought boxes of jewels out. The haggling seemed to go on for ages but eventually Tim bought 30 zircons and 12 sapphires.

After a cup of tea in a nearby café it was time to visit Buckingham Palace. I thought the palace was amazing, much bigger than I expected. We came across a hotdog stall and ate one each, followed by a strawberry milkshake in another café.

When it got dark we went to Piccadilly Circus. I was amazed by the lights, especially the big Coca Cola one. "I've never seen anything like it, it's magical," I gasped.

"If you like it you'd better take a good look," said Tim, grabbing my hand. I tried to wriggle free, but he wouldn't let go as we crossed the road to sit down by the Eros fountain. I looked at the signs for Wrigley's, Max Factor, Gordon's Gin and all the others. Red buses and black cabs whizzed past. I felt desperate not to miss anything as my eyes darted from sight to sight.

"Well, I'm tired if you're not," said Tim. "We need to find somewhere to sleep."

I already knew we were to sleep in the van as Tim wouldn't pay for somewhere to stay. "Is there a toilet around?" I asked as he drove along a quiet road.

"You should have asked earlier," he said, sounding annoyed. "You can go in the curb." I didn't want to, but I was bursting. "No one's any the wiser, are they?" he said as I pulled up my knickers.

"You can sleep up the front," he said, giving me my pillow and blanket. "It's best if I sleep in the back near the door. Go to sleep, we'll be up early again tomorrow."

I took off my top clothes but kept my vest and shorts on. I put my head on the pillow and used the blanket to cover myself up. It wasn't long after I'd settled that I heard Tim get in the back of the van. I instinctively kept quiet and pretended to be asleep. Utter exhaustion meant I soon was.

"What time is it?" I asked when Tim woke me up.

"It's six o'clock," he whispered.

"But it's not properly light yet."

Tim laughed. "We need to get moving before people get up. I'll take you to a cafe where you can have breakfast and tidy up. Then we'll spend another day sightseeing."

I really wanted to go home but part of me was keen to see the sights. "You can tell your friends about it," said Tim, as if reading my thoughts.

After breakfast we went to Selfridges where I tried to find a present for Mum, but couldn't afford anything. We went to an enormous Woolworths, much bigger than the one I was used to, then to Covent Garden, where I found a beautiful brooch for Mum. It was really pretty with feathers on it.

The rest of the day went by quickly as Tim took me to see Big Ben, Trafalgar Square, Tower Bridge and the Tower of London. That night he said we were going to sleep just outside London so he could get a better rest. He spotted somewhere after driving a few miles. "That looks as good a place as any," he said, pulling onto a grass verge. "It's quiet here, not much traffic."

As we prepared to drive off early next morning an old couple approached the van. The lady tapped on the window. "Are you all right, my dear?" she asked.

I nodded.

"You look very young."

"Wind down the window," said Tim from the back. "Of course she's all right," he snapped at the couple once the window was open. "She's my little sister."

The couple looked at us closely. "Now you mention it, I can

see the similarities," said the man. "Sorry about that."

"We were just worried about the girl, that's all," said the lady.

I felt sorry as they walked away because part of me wanted to go with them. "That's your fault for drawing attention to yourself," Tim snapped at me.

"I didn't mean to."

We went to a garage to freshen up and buy sandwiches. "We'll have a bite to eat before looking around," he said.

"What are we looking at?"

"Houses, and don't you dare draw attention to us."

"I won't."

When we'd eaten, Tim drove around before pulling in close to some lovely looking properties. "Right, you'll have to be quiet," he told me as he took out his binoculars. "It looks like the bloke is getting in his car to go to work." He glanced at his watch while I stayed silent. "Now you see why I wanted to be up early?"

I felt uneasy and said nothing as we waited a while longer.

"I'm feeling too hot sitting in the van, Tim," I finally moaned, hoping he would move on.

"What did I tell you? I told you to shut your mouth, didn't I?"

"Yes, but I don't like it here, I'm too hot."

"Well you'll have to put up with it and bloody well wait."

I kicked my sandals off as he continued looking intently at the house. "There's more movement. I think it's the old lady going out," he said as another car came down the drive.

"I'm bored, can't we go?" I asked.

Tim flew into a rage. "Be quiet, you spoilt brat. I'm trying to size things up, so shut up moaning."

I was too scared to say anymore. I ran my foot along the van floor. A sudden, sharp pain made me cry out in agony.

"What the hell's the matter with you now?"

"Something stung my foot," I squealed.

Tim glanced down towards my feet. "Looks like a wasp sting, that's the trouble with taking off your sandals"

I started crying.

"You can bloody well stop that," he said.

"But my foot hurts and I've got a terrible pain in my tummy."

"You stupid bitch, you're messing everything up. I shouldn't have brought you."

I flinched as Tim shouted at me with such ferocity that spittle landed on my face. "Do you want me to take you to the hospital?"

I shook my head and pleaded with tears streaming down my face, "No, just take me home, Tim; please."

"I suppose I'll have to, there's no point in staying here. Don't you dare expect me to bring you again. I don't know what in the hell Sam's going to say."

I felt too ill, too upset to answer back. "It's only a wasp bite, what a fuss," he snapped. I rubbed my stomach in an attempt to ease my pain. "Stop putting it on," he said. "It's all because you want to go home."

"It's not," I said. "I'm in agony."

The pain was excruciating so I curled up on my seat hoping to ease it as we drove home. Once we reached the motorway Tim speeded up. "No point in hanging around," he muttered. I continued crying silently and had a tear stained face by the time we got home.

"What's up, love?" asked Dad as I ran sobbing into his arms.

"A wasp stung her foot," Tim told him. "She's been kicking up such a fuss I've had to bring her home."

Dad looked concerned and bathed my foot, which was red and swollen. I told him I had stomach pains too and he suggested I have some milk and go to bed. Tim tried to tell Sam how I'd ruined everything, but he was sympathetic.

"She can't help being stung by a wasp, Tim," said Sam as he gave me a wink. "The main thing is that you're okay isn't it, my beauty?"

"Tell Mum I love her and I'll see her tomorrow," I told Dad as I went to bed.

"I will. You have a good sleep, love."

I felt so relieved to be home and able to sleep in my own bed.

* * *

I felt a lot better the next morning, but Tim was still furious and got frustrated with Dad and Sam when they tried to defend me. I was so happy when Mum managed a smile when I gave her the brooch. "I liked the sights of London but I'm glad to be home," I told her, taking her hand. "A wasp stung my foot. It's sore, Mum."

"Sore," she whispered.

I was surprised to hear her speak and hugged her. "Yes, but not as sore as it was yesterday."

She seemed pleased and I sat with her until she fell asleep, before returning to my room to read.

"We need a loaf, Christine. Come up the shops with me so

you can nip in and get it," Tim called up the stairs.

I sighed and put my book down. "I'm on my way," I called out.

We were soon parked up outside the shop, and when I came out with the bread I was shocked to see Tim arguing with the village policeman.

"Get in," Tim snapped at me as he revved the engine.

The policeman was determined not to let Tim go and stuck his boot under a wheel of the van. I was frightened as Tim revved the engine even harder, making it roar. The policeman looked more determined not to let Tim go and started telling him off about his driving. Tim revved the engine yet again until it screamed and the van took off, going right over the policeman's toes.

I gasped in alarm and was scared stiff as he swung the van around in the village square, the tyres squealing. People were looking out of their windows to see what was happening. By the time we got back the policeman had walked across the road and was standing outside his house. Tim braked hard and skidded to a stop right beside him, the policeman jumping out of the way and looking badly shaken.

"You'd better leave me alone, copper," snarled Tim angrily. I cringed. The policeman tried to reason with Tim but he looked crazy. "Leave me alone," he said. "Don't forget, I know you've got kids."

The policeman's face went white as a sheet and I felt really sorry for him as Tim revved up and sped away.

"I don't think you should have gone over the policeman's toe,

Tim," I said.

"How dare you side up with a copper" He gave me a nasty glare and began swerving from one side of the road to the other. "I'll bloody well throw you out," he yelled, leaning across the front of me and opening the van door. I held on to my seat as tightly as I could. "Don't, Tim! Don't push me out!" I screamed.

He laughed. "I bloody well will if you go against me again."

I almost wet myself with fear. When we got home I ran up to my room and prayed to God that police would come and arrest him by the end of the day. All week, I felt sure it wouldn't be long before Tim got arrested for what he had done, but no one came. In the end, I just wished he would die.

Some weeks later we heard the policeman had left the village. When Dad asked Aunty Alice about it, she said she believed he'd put in for a transfer. I was more terrified of Tim than ever.

Chapter Twenty-Six

THE BIG NEWS when we returned to school after the Easter break was that Wendy was going out with the boy from the shoe shop. Maureen had seen them on the bus together, and Wendy confirmed it over what had become our usual lunch at the chip-shop.

"He's called Tommy and he's ever so nice," she said. "We went to the cinema."

"Did he kiss you?" asked Maureen.

"I bet he did," teased Hazel. "And that you sat in the back seat with him."

"We might have, but you'll have to guess," laughed Wendy.

"We'll ask him. Won't we Maureen?" said Hazel with a grin.

Wendy glared at us. "Don't you dare. I'll never speak to you again."

"I'm sure she'll tell us when she's ready," I said.

After we'd eaten, we went to Woolworths for a drink, then stood in awe as Wendy went into the shoe shop. She and Tommy chatted before he walked her to the door. "We're still on for Friday evening, aren't we?" he said.

"Yes, I'll meet you at the same place, same time," said Wendy.

We begged her to tell us where this meeting place was.

"It's outside The Singing Kettle if you must know," she told us after a while.

"You lucky devil," said Hazel. "I'm told they've got a juke box."

"We'll all have to go one evening," said Wendy.

I felt sad, knowing Tim would never let me. His presence – whether he was actually there or not – was casting a huge shadow over every aspect of my life.

He came up to my room the next time Dad was working nights and Sam had gone out. "You can see Mum's getting worse," he said after abusing me. I didn't want to hear it. "We'll get somewhere together after she dies," he went on. He actually sounded happy, and I knew protesting wouldn't do any good, so I kept quiet.

Desperation overwhelmed me once he'd left my room. There seemed to be no escape from his vile plan. I couldn't go on and thought maybe I should kill myself. But a little voice inside my head told me I shouldn't. I wanted to tell someone, get help. But after his behaviour with the policeman I was sure Tim had no fear, sure too that he would get his guns and shoot Mum and wipe out the whole family if I even uttered a word.

I sat up all night, asking myself over and over, "What can I do? What can I do?" I decided I would have to be brave and tell Dad. I felt he'd understand if I explained how Tim had threatened to kill me, Mum and all the family.

A week passed before I finally got some time on my own with him, and with my heart beating hard in my chest I summoned all my courage.

"Dad," I said.

"What is it my dear?"

"I'm... I'm having problems with Tim, Dad." At last I began blurting it all out. "He's been making me get undressed and... and he's been doing things to me. I need to get away from him, Dad. He's threatened to kill me and Mum if I dare tell anyone."

Dad looked shocked; crushed. I continued.

"He's even said he'll kill you, Sam and Aunty Alice and Uncle Will too."

I could see Dad believed me as I watched him digest what I'd said, my heart still beating like never before. It looked as if he was making a plan.

"Christine," he said finally. "Do you think you could put up with it for a little while longer, love?"

I couldn't believe what he had just asked me, and he clearly sensed my shock. "Just until I save enough money for you to get away"

My heart sank to my boots. Was I hearing him right? I'd expected Dad to help me right away. But he wasn't going to. He couldn't do it.

I wanted to scream at him. I wanted to yell, "No! Oh no Dad, I can't stand it for another moment!" Instead I very quietly said, "Yes."

"I'll sort it out for you," he assured me.

Several weeks went by without Dad saying any more about it. I began to feel terribly let down and desperate. Mum was getting more and more poorly, and I knew that if anything happened to her, Tim would take me as far away as he could. I wondered if I should confide in Sam but worried he might start abusing me too. I was in a state of utter turmoil. My situation seemed hopeless.

One Saturday afternoon Sam said he was going into town to pick up some records he had ordered. "Could I come with you, Sam?" I asked.

"Do you mind if she goes, boy?" he asked Tim. I pushed my fingernails into the palms of my hands, but fortunately Tim agreed.

"I suppose so," he said. "But I want help with pumping the bellows when you come back, Christine."

I was still trying to decide whether or not to tell Sam as I got into the van, then suddenly it all came out. "Sam, I've got something I need to tell you," I blurted.

"What's up?" he asked. "I was thinking that you're not your usual self."

"It's Tim. I'm... I'm having problems with him. He's making me get undressed." I stared at Sam, terrified what his reaction would be. He looked shocked and pulled over to the side of the road.

"He's what?"

"Making me undress," I repeated. "When Dad's working nightshift and you go out."

"How long has this been going on?"

"A long time, I can't remember exactly."

"Why didn't you say before?"

I started crying. "I was afraid to. Tim said if I did, he'd kill Mum and me."

"The bastard"

"He said he'd shoot us all if I said anything."

Sam put his arm around me.

"He wants us to live together like man and wife when Mum dies," I said, sobbing uncontrollably.

"I was beginning to think his behaviour was getting a bit odd," said Sam almost to himself. "The way he won't let you go out or do anything."

I nodded.

"What do you want to do about it?"

"I don't know," I said, my face soaked in tears. "I just want to get away from him."

"Do you want to go to the police station so you can report it?"

I nodded again.

"But if I take you, promise me you won't mention anything about the guns."

"I promise, Sam."

"Because Tim and me, we'll be sent to prison. Do you understand?"

Again I nodded.

"Okay, let's go then. I think it's the only thing we can do. This situation can't continue. Just tell them the same as you told me."

I felt a huge wave of relief, which was replaced by fear as we parked outside the police station. I could feel myself shaking as Sam led me up to the desk. "My sister has something to report," he told the officer.

"It's all right, my dear. I'll get one of the lady officers to see you," said the policeman. He sounded kind and I felt a bit better. "Give me your sister's details please, Sir," he said.

Sam gave him my name and address, which he wrote in his notebook. "Sit down and I'll get someone to see you," he told us.

Sam and I sat and waited. I tried desperately to summon all my courage.

"Christine?" I jumped to my feet as I heard my name called out, and Sam stood up beside me.

"Are you Christine?" asked a lady officer.

"Yes."

"Follow me, dear."

She led us along a corridor and into a room, where she asked me to take a seat. Another female officer joined us.

"So what is it you want to report, Christine?" the first woman asked.

I knew I had to force myself to speak up. "My... my brother's been making me get undressed and... and he's been touching my private parts," I stammered.

I felt myself flush up as I said it. The lady officers looked at Sam.

"He's two years younger than me," he said.

"How old are you Christine?" one of them asked.

"I'm fifteen I'll be sixteen in November."

They exchanged glances. "How old is your brother?"

"Twelve years older than me," I said.

"He's twenty-seven," Sam told them.

They exchanged glances again. "How often has he been making you get undressed?"

"I'm not sure, I've lost count." They looked shocked. "It's usually on a Saturday night when Dad's working nightshift and Sam goes out," I said. "Mum's in bed."

"Mother had a stroke and she's bedridden," Sam explained. They nodded and asked how long it had been going on. I tried to think.

"Do you remember how old you were when it first began?" one of them asked.

"I must have been eleven or twelve at the time."

Sam was horrified. "You mean it's been happening all this time?" he said.

"Why haven't you said something about it before, Christine?" a policewoman asked.

"Because Tim threatened to kill me and Mum if I dared tell anyone," I said, bursting into tears again. "He... he said... he said he'd strangle me and suffocate Mum."

I wanted to tell them about the guns and his threats to shoot us all, but I'd promised Sam.

"Could you tell us about it, Christine?" one of the female officers asked. "Tell us how it started."

I wiped tears from my eyes and tried to compose myself.

"Are you able to remember it, Christine?" the other lady officer asked.

I coughed to clear my throat and nodded. "Yes, I remember it very well," I told her. "It was a Sunday night because Tim was helping me wash my hair so I'd be ready for school next morning."

I could see they were listening intently, nodding their heads. "I suddenly felt Tim pressing up again me," I went on, sniffling and wiping away more tears. "I didn't know what he was doing or why he was doing it. I found it annoying."

I stopped speaking because the memory was so painful.

"Take your time," one of the officers said gently.

"Tim... Tim ordered me to go upstairs and get undressed. I... I felt sick. I told him I didn't want to get undressed and begged him not to make me."

I began crying again. I was aware they were writing down every word I said. "My legs went shaky, I... I felt weak. I kept protesting that I didn't want to get undressed, but... but this made Tim angry."

"What do you mean by angry?" the other officer asked.

"He pushed me up the stairs and threatened to kill me if I didn't," I sobbed. "He hit me across the ear when I wouldn't get undressed and pulled all my clothes off."

I looked towards Sam and he looked back at me in shock.

"What happened after that?" they asked when they'd finished writing.

I stared at the floor in silence.

"Go on, Christine, take your time," said one of the officers.

"Tim made me..." I couldn't get the words out as I sat there crying, my shoulders shaking.

"It is okay, Christine. Just take your time."

"He... he made me open my legs... so he could see my private parts, and..."

"And what Christine?"

"And then he started touching me." I sobbed even more. I felt as if I'd bared my soul and wished the ground would swallow me up.

"You're a brave girl for managing to tell us this," said one of the officers.

"Thanks for bringing her in," the other said to Sam.

"Wait here, we need to discuss this," the first officer told us.

Sam and I were left alone in the room. I felt awful about having said it all in front of him. He appeared shattered.

"I had no idea, I'll kill him," he said angrily.

The officers soon returned. "We've decided it wouldn't be right to send Christine home," they told Sam, who nodded in agreement. "Do you know anyone who could put her up for the night?" Sam looked surprised. "It's only until the morning when social services will step in."

"Yes, I suppose we could ask Mrs Hendy, couldn't we?" Sam looked at me.

"Yes," I agreed. I felt sure that once Tim knew I'd told the police he'd want to kill me. Sam gave Mrs Hendy's phone number and address to the police officers and they rang her and she agreed I could stay.

"We'll take her round. You can go home," they said to Sam.

He looked concerned. "There'll be hell let loose when I get home," he told them.

"The main thing is to keep Christine safe; don't let him know where she is."

"No, I won't do that." He turned to me as we walked towards the police car. "Don't worry. I'll dismantle the van if I have to. I won't let him come after you."

"Thanks, Sam," I said as I got into the car. He gave me a wave and I managed to wave back as I was driven away.

By the time I arrived at Mrs Hendy's I felt as if my heart was breaking.

"All right, dear?" she said as she gave me a hug.

"Yes, thanks," I whispered.

Mrs Hendy told me her daughter had said I could sleep in her room that night.

"You'll be all right, she'll look after you," she said.

"Thank you," I said again.

"Social services will be around to collect her in the morning between 9 and 9.30. I know it's a Sunday, but they've an out of hours' team at weekends," the policewoman told Mrs Hendy.

She nodded. "Make sure they're not late, won't you?" she urged them. "The last thing we want is Tim around here."

"Any problems, dial 999."

Mrs Hendy put her arm round me when they'd left. "What a thing to happen to you," she said. I felt choked up and just nodded my head. "I've got chicken broth left over, would you like some?"

"Yes please," I said. I wasn't hungry but I didn't want to be rude.

Tucked up in bed I couldn't sleep for worrying what would

happen to me in the morning. I was worrying about Sam, too, and how he would manage to tell Tim about what had happened. I knew he'd be furious when Sam returned home without me.

Chapter Twenty-Seven

I WAS READY and waiting when a man and lady from social services arrived to pick me up the next morning. "It's all right, love," said Mrs Hendy, squeezing my hand. "I'm sure they'll do what's best for you."

Tears welled in my eyes. "Take care, my dear," said Mrs Hendy as I left.

"We'll make sure she's all right," the female social worker assured her.

"We're taking you to a children's home, Christine," said the man.

"Thank you," I replied.

"Have you got any other clothes?" asked the lady.

"No."

"It's all right, we'll arrange for someone to get your things. We're taking you to Newquay."

As we began driving away from Mrs Hendy's, my thoughts turned to Mum.

"Are you all right, Christine?" the lady asked.

"Yes, just worried about my mum," I said.

She nodded. "I think someone told me she's bedridden, is that right?"

"Yes, she's had another stroke."

"We'll see how she is when we collect your clothes," she told me.

"Thank you," I said.

I was amazed when the car pulled up to a large house with steps leading up to the front door. "This is it," said the man, opening the door for me to get out.

I was nervous. I'd never been to such a posh place before. Everything looked immaculate. The floor in the entrance hall was so shiny I was afraid to walk on it in case I made it dirty. A lady polishing the banisters smiled at me.

"It's this way to the office," the lady social worker said.

We got to a door marked MATRON and the social worker knocked. We walked into the office and the social worker said, "This is Christine who we telephoned about."

Matron, a kindly looking lady wearing a navy-blue dress with her hair tied back in a bun, smiled at me. "Welcome to Trenance, Christine," she said. "So, you're coming to stay with us for a while?"

I felt out of my depth. "Yes." I said.

She patted my arm gently. "You'll be all right here with us"

I did my best to smile at her as the male social worker handed my file over.

"Thanks," said Matron. "I suppose you'll keep us informed

about a court date?"

Court date? I hadn't even thought about going to court. Would Tim be sent to prison? None of this had entered my mind. I'd been so focused on getting away.

The social workers and Matron discussed going to Fir Tree to collect my things. "Is there anything you want in particular, Christine?" the lady social worker asked.

"My candy striped dress and tartan trews" I said.

The social workers promised they'd bring all they could before Matron offered to show me where I would be sleeping. I followed her up the stairs.

"You'll be in this dormitory," she said as she opened a door. I looked in at a large room with six beds in it.

"This will be your bed," said Matron walking towards it. "You can keep your things in here..." she pointed to a bedside cabinet before opening a wardrobe "... and hang your clothes in there."

"Thank you, Matron," I said, impressed by how clean and tidy it was.

She smiled kindly at me. "We'll be having lunch soon," she said, looking at her watch. "I'll show you the bathroom just along the corridor so you can freshen up."

I took a few moments to wash my hands and splash water on my face. I felt glad to have escaped Tim, but I missed Mum. A young member of staff met me on the stairs. "I'm Laura," she said. "I'm going to look after you."

She reminded me of Wendy and I suddenly missed my school friends and wondered if I would ever see them again.

It was cottage pie for lunch, which I was really pleased about.

I sat at a table with Laura, who introduced me to the other girls. After we'd eaten, Laura asked if I'd like to take a walk to a nearby park.

"Yes please," I said, looking out at the sunshine.

We spent a lovely hour there with some of the younger children. When the social worker brought my clothes later that afternoon, Laura offered to help me put them away. After the evening meal I met a girl nearer my age called Muriel. We went into the lounge together to watch TV, but both of us were very quiet. The television was switched off at 9pm, and it was bedtime.

"Are you coming to school tomorrow?" asked Muriel.

I shook my head. "No one's mentioned it," I told her.

She looked disappointed. "I expect they've got to sort it out before you do," she said. I nodded.

Most of the children – there must have been around 40 in all, many of them younger than me – were asleep by the time I got into bed. I tried to get off to sleep but was kept awake by the sound of someone crying. I felt sad myself and began to cry quietly into my pillow. I was worried about going to court and wondered what would happen. Eventually I fell asleep, worn out by the anguish.

* * *

Several days went by and I started getting used to the routine. I felt happier having discovered there was a library at the home, and that's where I was when a care worker came to tell me my father had arrived. I jumped up in excitement and followed her along the corridor to the visitor's room. She opened the door and

I stopped dead. It was Tim.

"It's all right, it's all right," he said. But the care worker must have realised something was wrong, seen the horror on my face.

"Is he not your dad, Christine?"

"No!" I screamed, "It's my brother, Tim."

His face darkened with rage and I was terrified he'd kill me. I don't know if the care worker pressed an alarm bell, but other members of staff soon came running in and two men grabbed Tim and held him by the arms. He glared angrily at me, struggling as they dragged him away.

"I was only looking after you," he yelled, looking back towards me as they reached the door. "You'll end up a prostitute, that's what'll happen to you."

I felt sick with fear. The care worker tried to reassure me that Tim had gone. Laura appeared and put her arm around me.

"How did he find out where I was?" I asked. No one knew. I was taken to Matron's office.

"I'm sorry, Christine. We all thought it was your father," she said. "Your social worker said she told your dad where you were, so we thought he'd come to see you."

I shook my head. "My dad's afraid of Tim too, he must have told him."

Matron looked annoyed. "That's bad," she said. "Don't worry, it won't be allowed to happen again. I'll inform the police."

A few days later Dad did arrive. After Matron had asked me to verify who he was, I gave him a hug. He looked flustered. "I'm sorry about Tim coming here," he muttered.

"I was terrified." I said.

He nodded. "Let's go out for a little walk, you can show me around the garden."

As soon as Dad felt sure we couldn't be heard, he stopped and faced me. "You know when you go to court, Christine?" he said.

"Yes."

"Well, you won't mention anything about guns, will you?"

"No, of course not, I promised Sam I wouldn't."

Dad nodded. "It's just, if you do, Tim will be sent to prison. There won't be anyone to look after Mum. You wouldn't want that, would you?"

"No of course not"

"Promise me then"

"I promise I won't"

He looked relieved. "That's good," he said. "I don't want to see Tim sent away"

"It's all right, I won't say anything"

He needed a lot of reassurance, but finally seemed satisfied by what I'd said, and we continued our walk through the gardens. Looking back, it was emotional blackmail really, ensuring I didn't reveal the full truth. I felt I couldn't let my family down, so I had to keep quiet. I'd promised Sam and promised Dad. I feared they'd never forgive me if I broke those promises.

As we walked back, I remained silent all the way, waiting for Dad to give me a sign that he still loved me and he cared about what happened to me. None came.

Back in the house he told Matron the gardens were beautiful. Then he hugged me and left. I asked Matron if I was going back to school.

"I'm not sure, Christine. Your social worker's taking you for a medical examination tomorrow morning." I was confused. "Have a nice bath when you get up," she said.

Laura ran me a bath the next morning and I felt nice and clean when I put on my candy-striped dress. Laura said she liked it. After breakfast, a social worker arrived and introduced herself as Miss Lewis. When we got in the car, she asked me how things were, and I said I was missing my friends and wanted to go back to school.

"You won't be able to until after the court case," said Miss Lewis. "We have to wait and see what the court decides."

I must have looked bewildered. "That's why I'm taking you for a medical," she explained. "You understand what's happening, don't you?"

I shook my head.

"You mean no one's told you?" she asked.

"Told me what?"

"That you're seeing a police doctor for an internal examination."

I was shocked and was shaking by the time we arrived at the hospital.

"Do as you're told and it won't take long," whispered Miss Lewis.

"Get undressed and slip on this gown," said a nurse, pointing to a cubicle. I did as she said. "Are you ready?" she asked, looking in.

"Yes," I said. I followed her until she knocked on a door.

"Come in," a man's voice answered. When the door opened I saw a police lady and a man standing around a bed.

"Christine," said the nurse as a form of introduction before leaving me with them.

"Get on the bed, Christine," said the police lady.

Reluctantly I did it as the doctor put on a pair of white rubber gloves.

"You'll have to open your legs, Christine," said the police lady.

I froze. I couldn't to do it. "Do as you're told," she said impatiently.

"We'll have to use stirrups," suggested the doctor.

She nodded in agreement. "You wouldn't be kicking up this much fuss if it was your brother doing it would you?" she said impatiently.

I felt distressed and hated that she could think that.

"You liked it when your brother was doing it didn't you?" she said.

"No! I hated it, I hated it," I screamed at her.

She looked shocked but nodded. "Sorry, it's just I had to ask," she said apologetically.

"This won't take long," said the doctor as he put my feet in the stirrups. I braced myself to endure it.

"There you are, it didn't hurt, did it?" said the doctor afterwards.

"No," I said, jumping off the bed. I ran back to the cubicle, got dressed and went outside to find Miss Lewis. I asked her when the court case would be, but she didn't know.

"It all depends how long the reports and medical results take," she said. "Sometimes they're quite quick, other times they take longer."

"I hope they're quick," I said. "My friends will wonder where I am."

"Your school has been informed," said Miss Lewis.

"Oh," I said.

She smiled at me. "It must be a lot for you to deal with."

I nodded. "I'm worried about the court case and seeing Tim."

She tried to reassure me, but I was upset and embarrassed about being examined.

Back at the home, I couldn't eat my lunch. I felt unwell and lay in bed. When I woke up it was teatime and I felt a bit better. We ate and I went to the library and chose a book to read, selecting David Copperfield.

Chapter Twenty-Eight

I BURST INTO tears. Several anxious weeks had gone by and now, finally, Miss Lewis was telling me the court date was fixed. She gave me her handkerchief and I sobbed into it until it was soaking wet. "I'm worried stiff," I managed to say.

She did all she could to try and make me feel better, but I was terrified the court would send me home. I knew I'd have to run away if they did. I couldn't live with Tim again.

The day arrived and I couldn't face breakfast. "I hope it all goes well for you," said Matron, touching my arm. "Be a brave girl and speak up."

Waiting in the car was a Mrs Martin, and as we drove, she and Miss Lewis began to chat. "Where do you think he's most likely to be?" Mrs Martin asked Miss Lewis.

"He'd try to stop us on the Goss Moor, no doubt," said Miss Lewis quietly. "I must do my best not to stop we can't let him take her."

My stomach knotted as I put two and two together – Tim

was going to try and grab me. I shuddered and clung to my seat. I was petrified as we crossed Goss Moor, and so relieved when we didn't see him.

"I think we should be all right now," said Miss Lewis as we entered town.

"Yes, less likely to happen here," said Mrs Martin.

"At least we're here in good time, Christine," said Miss Lewis, glancing back at me after parking the car.

The three of us walked into court. Miss Lewis made her way to the desk, and I stood beside her as she gave my name. The man referred to his list. "Your case is booked in for Court Room 3 and down for 11 o'clock" he said. "Take a seat in the waiting area. When you're needed you'll be called."

My heart was racing as we sat down. I dried my hands with a tissue because my palms were getting clammy.

"Don't forget to speak up and answer questions clearly," Miss Lewis reminded me.

"We'll be sitting beside you; you've got nothing to fear," added Mrs Martin.

"We shouldn't be long now," said Miss Lewis looking at her watch. I felt panicky but fought to hold it back. I knew how important it was to be brave.

When the time came, I walked in a haze as Miss Lewis guided me along the corridor. A man opened the door for us and we took a seat, Miss Lewis and Mrs Martin on either side of me as they'd promised. I spotted my father and Tim sitting on benches on the other side of the room. They looked at me nervously. Sam wasn't with them and I decided he must be at work.

There were three serious looking people sitting at the front of the room, a man with a woman either side of him. Their desk towered above me. The man spoke, "So, we're deciding today on a case of sexual abuse."

The court room went quiet and I felt uneasy as everyone looked at me until my father was called up to speak. He made excuses for my brother, saying he was a good son who'd stayed home to look after his mother after she'd had a stroke. People looked sympathetic as he explained how she was bedridden and couldn't do anything for herself. Tim wasn't asked to say anything but sat looking embarrassed.

After a bit of discussion, the man and two ladies looked at me. I felt dreadful under their gaze. I stood up.

"Could you tell us a bit of what's been happening, Christine?" said the man.

Before I'd said a word, one of the ladies spoke. "What sort of things did Tim do to you?"

I felt extremely scared and embarrassed but forced myself to speak up. "He... he made me undress and... and looked at my private parts," I stuttered.

"What else did he do? Did he do anything else?" the other lady asked.

"He made... he made me put my bottom up on a pillow and... and started touching me. He threatened if I didn't let him do it, he'd kill me and Mum."

I heard one of the ladies gasp. "I think that's enough questioning," the man in the middle said. I felt my face burning and I knew I must have gone bright red. I was told I could sit down.

I looked nervously across at Dad and Tim. Dad was looking uneasy and Tim completely embarrassed. The man and the two ladies got up and went to a back room, leaving the rest of us in the room together for about ten minutes. I was relieved to have the protection of the two social workers. "It'll soon be over," whispered Miss Lewis in my ear.

"Stand, everyone," said an authoritative voice.

The three entered the room before the man tapped on the desk.

"We've come to a decision," he said. I held my breath. "We've decided it wouldn't be right to send Christine back home. We're placing her in the care of Cornwall County Council in need of care and protection."

I was overcome by relief. I avoided looking at Dad and Tim as I was quickly led out. "It's over," said Miss Lewis. "You must be pleased?"

"I am," I said. I knew nothing about the law. It might not have even been a full court hearing, just one held by social services. All I knew was that I wanted to get away from Tim.

In the car, Mrs Martin asked if I was glad. I told her I was, but that I'd miss my mum. She told me that something would be sorted out.

I was quiet during the drive back to the children's home. Matron was pleased to hear the news and said a decision would soon be made about where I would be living.

A week later, she told me I was being sent to a girls' home in Plymouth to keep me safe from Tim. I was glad and quite excited to be getting further away from him. When the time came, I said goodbye to Laura and Matron and got into the car with Miss Lewis and Mrs Martin.

* * *

"Welcome to Woodside. I'm Miss Wilkins."

"Thank you," I said.

Miss Wilkins spoke to my social workers. "We've decided to keep Christine over here in the big house," she told them. "We feel it would be safer."

"That sounds wise," said Miss Lewis.

"You don't mind do you, staying in a mother-and-baby home?" Miss Wilkins asked me. "It's only for a while. You'll be able to go across the road to the girls' home later."

I didn't mind. I was happy just to feel safe.

Miss Wilkins smiled at me. "Is that all the clothing Christine's got?" she asked, looking at my bag.

"Yes, we'll apply for a clothing grant as soon as we get back," said Miss Lewis, before she and Mrs Martin left having promised to be in touch. I felt quite lost without them.

A Mrs Mann showed me to the dormitory where there were four beds. "You'll be sharing with Shirley as well as Susan and Beryl, who are both expectant mums," she said.

She showed me the bathroom. "Go careful with the hot water in the morning," she said. "It's needed by the expectant mums. If they have a hospital appointment, they want a bath."

Back downstairs, Mrs Mann took me into the dining room and introduced me to Susan, who would be looking after me.

"How old are you?" she asked as soon as I sat down.

"I'm fifteen."

"The same as me," she said. "You're not pregnant, are you?"

I shook my head. "No, I've been taken into care," I told her, repeating what I'd heard them say in court. She didn't look surprised.

Susan and I chatted as we ate. She told me she was four months pregnant.

"Oh," I said.

"It's all right, you must think I'm too young," she said noticing my awkwardness. I blushed. "My parents were furious when they found out, that's why I'm here."

"Oh," I said again. "Wouldn't they let you stay at home?"

"No chance. They said I'd let the family down. Worse still, I've got to have my baby adopted when it's born." She looked really sad.

"I'm sorry," I said, and she smiled at me.

The food was great and afterwards Susan showed me around. Once again there were nice gardens to enjoy. I could hear a baby crying. "The babies are put outside so they can get plenty of fresh air," Susan explained. "They're at the back where the kitchen staff can keep an eye on them. There are six at the moment and two are expected soon."

Susan asked why I'd been taken into care. She seemed shocked when I told her about Tim. I said I'd rather not talk about it and she understood.

"Would you like to go on the swings?" she asked.

"I haven't been on a swing for ages," I said as we stopped

beside them.

"Go on then, I'll give you a push."

I felt a sense of freedom on the swing. It was lovely.

We went back indoors and up to our room. Shirley was there putting on nail varnish. Susan introduced us and explained Shirley was going out with her boyfriend Ben, that evening.

"He's in the Army but tonight's his night off," said Shirley. "We're going to the pictures, so Miss Wilkins said I can stay out late."

"What time have you got to be in?" asked Susan.

"Ten o'clock instead of half past nine," said Shirley just as the dinner bell rang.

"I'm starting work early tomorrow," said Shirley as we sat down for tea.

"What do you do?" I asked.

"I work as a chambermaid in a hotel on The Hoe."

I thought it was great. "I'd like to get a job," I said as our meals arrived.

"You're too young, aren't you?" said Susan. "When do you leave school?"

"I was due to leave when we broke up for summer."

"If that's the case, I doubt if you'll go back," said Shirley.

I felt sad. What had my friends been told? Were Wendy, Maureen and Hazel missing me? What was their news?

After dinner we went into the lounge to watch Coronation Street, a show I'd never seen before. There were about a dozen girls there, some of them older ladies who, I discovered, were unmarried mums. As Shirley left to meet Ben, one of the girls said, "Lucky devil, meeting her boyfriend."

"Wish it was me," said another.

Coronation Street started and everyone went quiet. Later, a member of staff came in with a trolley and offered us cocoa. It all felt very homely and comforting. I enjoyed my drink and it was soon time for bed. I had a wash, put on my nightdress and just as I was drifting off to sleep, Shirley came back.

"Ben's wonderful," she whispered. "I'm hoping we'll get engaged."

"Do you think you will?" I asked, sitting up.

She looked so happy. "Yes, I think so. We've been going out for six months."

"Be quiet you two," said Beryl. "I've got hospital in the morning."

"I'll tell you about it tomorrow," whispered Shirley. I plumped my pillow and fell asleep.

Chapter Twenty-Nine

MRS MANN TOLD me my clothing grant had arrived and that Mrs Brown, another care worker, would be taking me shopping that afternoon.

"Don't forget to be sensible, mind," she said. "Only buy clothes that are practical."

She'd come up to our dormitory to help us change our sheets. Susan told me that once a week we had to polish the cutlery too. I was surprised and enjoyed learning how to make a bed neat by using hospital corners.

Susan was sweetly envious of my shopping trip, so when I was called to the office after lunch I asked Mrs Brown if she could come with us. "Yes, I don't see why not – the more the merrier," she said.

Susan's face lit up. "Thanks, Mrs Brown," she said.

I felt really excited as Mrs Brown got her car keys. We went to the department store, Spooners, first where we made our way to ladies' fashion on the second floor. I chose a navy skirt and a black skirt in size eight and 10; the eight fitted perfectly. We looked for blouses next.

"This one's lovely, Christine," said Susan holding one up which had nice frills on the front.

"Not very practical though," Mrs Brown reminded us. "It's far too fancy for work."

Susan pulled a face and put it back.

"What about this white one?" said Mrs Brown taking it off the rail. "It would go well with your black or navy skirt."

I held it up for a better look. "Yes, it's quite nice," I said. "I'll have that one, I think."

Mrs Brown looked pleased. "Could I have this one as well?" I asked, spotting a nice pink one. Mrs Brown didn't look sure. "It would go well with my white skirt," I said hopefully.

She gave a smile. "I don't see why not," she said after checking the price. "You could have this cream one too," she added. "You could really do with three." I nodded in agreement.

Susan carried my clothes and we went to buy underwear and shoes. I chose three bras, some knickers and shoes that Susan had suggested. But I couldn't walk in them, so Mrs Brown selected some with a lower heel. I had some money left so I chose two cardigans, one black and the other pink.

Back at the home, Miss Wilkins was pleased with my purchases. I took my clothes up to the dormitory where Shirley was painting her nails again.

"I love your pink blouse," she said when I went to hang it up. "Can I try it on?"

She was wearing it before I had the chance to answer. "It fits me perfectly," she said looking in the mirror. "Can I borrow it to go out with Ben tonight?"

Not expecting to be asked, I stuttered awkwardly. "I'm... I'm not allowed to lend my clothes."

Shirley seemed annoyed as she took it off and handed it back. "Miss Wilkins wouldn't let me," I added.

"All right, don't make a fuss about it," said Shirley as Susan came in. She got ready and left without saying goodbye.

"What's up with her?" asked Susan after she'd gone.

"She wanted to borrow my new pink blouse and I wouldn't let her."

Susan nodded. "She tried the same with me. She wants to impress Ben."

"You think I did the right thing, then?" I asked.

"Of course you did. Miss Wilkins wouldn't like it."

I went to see Miss Wilkins the following morning. She looked pleased to see me as she welcomed me into her office.

"We need to make plans for your future," she said. "What do you want to do?" I hadn't expected to be asked and didn't know what to say. "Did you take any exams?"

"Yes, I took RSA English and Maths." Miss Wilkins wrote it down. "But I don't know what's going to happen now about getting my results."

"I'll get your school to send them here," said Miss Wilkins. "What did you plan to do after you left school?"

I felt awkward again and went red. "I don't know. My brother didn't want me to work. He wanted me to stay home with him." My own words sounded pathetic.

"Well, put it another way, what would you like to do now?" she asked.

"I'd like to learn shorthand and typing."

Miss Wilkins nodded her head. "That sounds good. I'll find out about classes if that's what you'd like."

"Yes please," I said, feeling happy.

"I think you'd do well in a nice little office job. Is there anything else?"

"Yes," I said. "What do we do if someone wants to borrow our clothes?"

"Has someone asked you?"

"Not really, it's just I thought I should know."

"We've a 'no-lending-or-borrowing' rule here," she said, her voice strict. "If anyone tells you differently refer them to me." I felt glad to hear it.

Miss Wilkins soon found shorthand and typing lessons for me three afternoons a week. I wrote and told Dad about it and he began writing to me. I looked forward to his letters to find out how Mum was. I think he must have felt guilty because on one occasion he enclosed a 10-shilling note (about 50p).

"I'm going to my shorthand lesson, Miss Wilkins," I said one afternoon.

"Good girl, see you later," she called out.

I was feeling quite light hearted as I went out the door. But I froze when I reached the pavement and saw Tim's van parked further along the road. He must have been looking out for me in the wing mirror because he jumped out of the van.

"Stop!" he yelled. "I wouldn't hurt you, Christine!"

I ran back into the home.

"I love you, I wouldn't hurt you," he called after me.

My heart was racing. He'd threatened to kill me so often that I didn't believe what he was saying.

"What's wrong, Christine?" asked Mrs Brown when she saw me return in a panic.

"I've just seen my brother Tim parked down the road in his van," I said, bursting into tears.

Miss Wilkins came out of her office and I told her what had happened. She looked angry and picked up the phone. "I'll call the police right away," she said. "This must be stopped."

By the time the police arrived Tim had disappeared. "We'll make sure he doesn't bother you again, my dear," said one of the policemen.

"They'll go to your house to see him if they don't catch him on the road," Miss Wilkins reassured me.

I was still feeling shaky so I didn't go to my class. The police rang the next morning and said they had spoken to Tim. I felt happier and grateful that they'd done so.

My school exam arrived soon after. I'd passed English and Maths and was interviewed for the position of credit clerk at Spooners, and I got the job. My life seemed to be moving forward at last, but life was falling apart for others at the home.

The sound of crying came from the dormitory as Susan and I returned from church one Sunday. We opened the door to find Trisha, one of the girls we were now sharing a room with, curled up on her bed sobbing as if her heart would break.

"Oh Trisha, what's wrong?" asked Susan as she sat beside

her.

"They're... they're taking my baby... tomorrow," she said between sobs and sniffles.

My heart went out to her. Susan put her arm around her and I caught hold of her hand. "I... I don't want them to. I'd like to keep her but... but my family won't let me."

"I know, I know," said Susan giving her a hug. "It's the same for me."

I was lost for words, feeling terribly sorry for both of them. We offered to take Trisha for a little walk.

"Yes, I think I might," she said. "Baby's in the nursery so I'll have to come back soon to feed her."

We strolled through the gardens, trying our best to talk about other things, anything but babies, to take her mind off it.

The following week Shirley and I were told we had to move across the road to Southview. Our beds were needed for new single mums coming into the home. I promised Susan I'd come back to see her.

Chapter Thirty

MISS DICKINSON, A friendly middle-aged woman with grey curly hair, answered the door at Southview. The first thing that caught my eye was the long, shiny passage which ran from the front of the bungalow to the back. The smell of lavender furniture polish hung in the air, reminding me of the polish Aunty Alice always used.

Once again we were in a dormitory, this time with six beds. Shirley bagged the one in the corner. As she unpacked, Miss Dickinson caught sight of a photo of Ben. Shirley was proud to tell her all about him. "Miss Wilkins let me go out with him on his nights off," she said.

Miss Dickinson nodded. "I don't mind you seeing him on his nights off."

Shirley sighed with relief. I thought how lucky she was. "You'll get a boyfriend soon, Christine," she said, as if she knew what I was thinking.

Sandy and Karen came into the room. Karen looked

interested as I unpacked my stuff. "What makeup do you have?" she asked.

"Just a couple of lipsticks and Max Factor Tempting Touch face powder."

She pulled a face. "We'll have to do something about that, won't we, Sandy?"

Sandy nodded. "We'll show you our makeup later," she said. "Do you have any nail varnish?"

"I've got a pink one." I took it out to show her.

She nodded and turned to Shirley. "You've got a nice lot of makeup, haven't you?"

Shirley shook her head. "Not much; Ben's not keen on it."

Karen looked surprised. "Boring, I haven't met a man yet who doesn't like makeup. Have you, Sandy?"

"No, never," laughed Sandy. "It's always the more makeup the better."

"Christine's got lovely skin, she doesn't need much makeup," interrupted Miss Dickinson. "So I don't want you two influencing her."

Karen turned around. "No, we wouldn't do that, would we, Sandy?" she asked in an innocent voice.

"No, we'll only give her a bit of advice, that's all," said Sandy, fixing her eyes on me. "You'll have to let me do your hair later, Christine. You'd look good with a bouffant."

"You could always brush it out again if you don't like it," Karen chipped in.

"Only if Christine wants you to," said Miss Dickinson firmly.

Both girls smiled at me. "You do don't you, Christine?" asked

Sandy. I nodded my head, pleased they wanted to help me.

"Would you like me to do your hair too, Shirley?" asked Sandy.

Shirley shook her head. "I'm going out with Ben tonight, another time maybe."

At dinner I met two more girls, Laura and Sally. Sandy said none of us should eat too much as we needed to think of our figures. I looked surprised.

"It's all right for you," she said, looking me over.

"I've never thought about it," I said.

Back in our room that evening, Sandy did my hair, teasing and backcombing it before spraying it with Karen's hairspray. I felt pleased when I looked at myself in the mirror. "I like it, I have to admit," I said.

Sandy smiled. "A big improvement isn't it, Karen?" Karen nodded, before Sandy asked, "Would you like to go to the youth club with us on Friday night?"

"I'd love to," I said. "What do we do there?"

"Play records, dance and have a game of table tennis," said Sandy.

"It gives us chance to meet some nice boys," added Karen with a grin.

"Will you do my hair before we go?" I asked Sandy.

"Yes and your makeup."

We went to show Miss Dickinson my hair. "Yes, it looks nice, Christine. But not for work, only going out," she said.

"Don't you think it makes her look more grown up, Miss Dickinson?" asked Laura.

"Yes, but that's not always a good thing."

As I'd promised, I didn't forget Susan, and asked her if she wanted to come with us to the youth club. She didn't, so I invited her to the cinema that coming Saturday.

When I was getting ready for the youth club that Friday, Sandy noticed my shoes. "They're nice," she said. "What a pity they won't fit me. I used to wear my mum's you know. She had beautiful shoes she wore out on the game."

Karen gave a whistle. "You shouldn't be telling people that."

"I don't care, I'm not ashamed of my mum," said Sandy defiantly, poking out her tongue. "There's nothing wrong with her being a working girl."

"Where does she work?" I asked. They both started laughing.

"She's a prostitute, silly," said Karen. I felt myself blush.

"She has to earn money somehow," said Sandy.

"Yes, but I doubt if Christine knows about that," said Karen.

"You know what a prostitute is don't you, Christine?" asked Sandy.

"Yes," I replied, remembering how Tim had said I'd become one.

"There you are, she knows," said Sandy sarcastically. Karen just shrugged her shoulders.

We said goodbye to Miss Dickinson and she reminded us to be back by 9.30pm. It was a great evening. I was out of practise but danced a twist to The Mashed Potato by Chubby Checker with a girl called Rosemary who'd recognised me from church.

A few weeks later, Karen and Sandy persuaded Miss Dickinson to let us attend an evening church service. They didn't tell me until we were out the door that they were actually planning to wander about looking for boys.

I wasn't keen on lying to Miss Dickinson. "It'll be alright, we've done it before," insisted Karen. "We'll be back by half nine."

"All right," I agreed. They both cheered.

"You won't regret it," said Sandy.

I felt bad as we headed down to the Barbican, which leads from Sutton Harbour up to Plymouth Hoe, with its cobbled streets of pubs, cafes, coffee bars, shops.

"We'll get a few matloes to buy us a drink," said Sandy.

I knew she was referring to sailors. "I don't know about that, surely it's not a good idea," I said.

They laughed. "It's a bit of fun, when we want rid of them we say we're going to the toilet," said Karen.

I was still nervous and worried when three boys bumped into us as they spilled out of a pub called The Friary. Sandy gave them a dirty look.

"Hey, gorgeous, where are you going tonight?" one of them shouted.

Sandy looked back. "Nowhere with you, so shove off."

They began following us, so we walked faster. I was quite amused by them and left Sandy to deal with it. When they wolf whistled at us Sandy swung around. "We don't want anything to do with you, so clear off."

They hurried to catch us up. "We're going to the Three Crowns for a drink," said Sandy, as one of them gave her a wink.

"That's funny," he said, "that's where we're going." Sandy

scowled. "We'll buy you a drink if you want one," said the boy.

Sandy and Karen smiled. "They could come along for a while couldn't they, Karen?"

Karen nodded. "All right, so what are you called?"

"I'm Andy and this is Dougie and Beano."

"I'm Sandy and this is Karen and Christine."

"What do you drink?" asked Andy.

Sandy and Karen said they'd have a Pony – I think it was a type of sherry – and suggested I have a Babycham. I'd not really drunk alcohol before, but for the port Aunty Mary used to give me when I had a cold.

I felt excited and quite grown up as we sat at a corner table waiting for the drinks. Andy came back from the bar and sat between me and Sandy. Dougie sat beside Karen and Beano sat at the other side of the table. Andy was the most talkative one and started telling us about his boat. I found it interesting when he began describing his fishing trips with his father. Dougie tried to get our attention by clowning around. I decided Dougie was boring but Karen thought him funny and was laughing at his silly jokes. When we finished our drinks they went back to the bar to buy us another.

"I think Dougie's nice, he's a bit of fun," said Karen.

"I prefer Andy," I said. "I've taken a liking to him."

Sandy smiled at me. "I'm not keen, they're not my type."

I was glad. I found myself liking Andy more and more, enjoying his easy-going chatter.

"We're going to have to go now," I told him when I saw it was nine o'clock.

"Where do you live? Let's walk you home," he said, jumping to his feet.

"At the girls' home in Woodside," said Sandy.

They all got up. "That's all right, I don't live far from there," said Andy.

Beano suddenly disappeared. Andy walked between Sandy and me while Dougie walked alongside Karen.

"What's happened to Beano?" said Sandy.

Andy and Dougie laughed. "Don't worry about him, he's always shoving off like that," said Andy.

We chatted all the way home. "When can we meet you again?" asked Andy when we reached Lipson Road.

"We could meet them on Wednesday, couldn't we?" I asked Sandy and Karen.

"Meet us by the horse trough at half-past seven," Karen told them.

"Don't forget to be there," they called out as we walked away. There was a chill in the late evening air, but I felt quite warm inside.

"They can forget that, I won't be meeting them," said Sandy right away.

"You'll meet Dougie won't you, Karen?" I asked.

She nodded as she rang the doorbell at Southview. "Yes, I suppose so; I might as well. Right, leave this to me," she said as the door opened. "We're sorry we're late Miss Dickinson, we stopped for a coffee."

"Have supper then get ready for bed," said Miss Dickinson, looking us over.

"Do you think she smelled drink on us?" whispered Karen.

Sandy shook her head. "No, she didn't suspect or she would have said."

The next day a new girl, Cathy, joined the home, and I was given the task of looking after her. I took her over the road to meet Susan. I couldn't wait to tell her about Andy, and Susan was pleased for me and asked me to let her know how I got on.

When Wednesday came around, Karen had broken her arm and was in hospital. I was upset she couldn't come, and more than a little nervous about going on my own, but I so wanted to see Andy again. I was determined not to let Tim ruin my life and assured myself that all boys/men weren't like him. I wanted to fall in love and get married, just like my cousin Victoria.

My heart started racing when I caught sight of Andy waiting at the horse trough. "Why isn't Karen with you?" asked Dougie when I got there.

"She's broken her arm and gone to the hospital."

He was clearly disappointed. "So where would you like to go?" asked Andy. "What about El Sombrero?"

"Yes if you like. I've never been there," I said. I knew it was a coffee bar and had a jukebox.

My heart skipped a beat as Andy took my hand before the three of us began walking.

Hello Mary Lou by Ricky Nelson was playing as we arrived at El Sombrero. "Want a cappuccino?" asked Andy after we'd found a table.

"I like it in here," I said as Andy and Dougie returned from the counter. "I love the red scarves and raffia-covered Chianti bottles hung on the walls."

"I can't say I really noticed," said Dougie looking up.

"That's because you're too busy looking at girls," laughed Andy.

Dougie delved into his pocket. "I think I'll put some music on," he said, and made his way to the jukebox.

"So, you like it here then?" Andy put his arm around me.

"It's really nice," I said, as Teen Angel started playing before Dougie came back and sat down.

"I was just about to tell her about your mother reading our tea leaves," Andy told him.

"Reading your tea leaves?" I was mystified.

Dougie shook his head and grinned.

"Before we met you on Sunday I had tea at Dougie's. His mother's a dab hand at reading tea leaves." I was fascinated. "She said we'd meet three girls didn't she, Dougie?"

"Yes, that's what she told us."

"She said I'd end up with two girls and Dougie with one," he added.

"That must have been me and Sandy," I said.

Andy nodded. "Yes, because Beano shoved off and Dougie paired up with Karen."

"How strange," I said. "Fancy her telling you that."

They both laughed. "That wasn't all though was it, Andy?" said Dougie.

"No, she said I'd stay with one girl and end up marrying her."

"So you see, you were in the tea leaves," Dougie told me with a grin.

I smiled at him. "Interesting, but I don't know about that," I said.

"It seemed strange that when we came out of The Friary, you three walked past," said Andy. I nodded my head. "Just like fate," he added. I couldn't help smiling.

"Do you two want another cup?" asked Dougie.

I looked at my watch. "Yes, I could manage one more."

As they went up to the counter, Buddy Holly's That'll be the Day came on. "I love this song," I said when they came back.

"Me too, I love Buddy Holly," said Dougie, with Andy nodding in agreement.

"So when can I see you again?" he asked as he walked me home.

I was keen to see him again and was pleased he'd asked. It was all very exciting. I'd just turned 16 and he was 18. "I'm going to the youth club on Friday if you'd like to go," I said.

He smiled at me. "Yes, it sounds all right, which one?"

"Kings Street"

"And you're sure it would be all right if I come along?"

"Yes, if you want." My words made his face light up. "Meet me at the horse trough at seven," I told him.

My heart was beating fast as I rang the doorbell. "You look flushed," said Miss Dickinson when she opened the door.

I nodded. "It's because I've been rushing, I didn't want to be late."

"You're a good girl," she said. "Not like some of the others." I felt myself blush and went to sleep thinking of Andy.

Sandy gave me a bouffant for youth club. "You look lovely,"

she said, as I stood admiring my new hairdo in the mirror in my black and white hounds tooth skirt, white nylon blouse and black cardigan and jacket. She, Karen and Cathy had decided to come with me, and I had butterflies of excitement as we left.

I squealed when I spotted Andy. I introduced him to Cathy; the other two were lagging behind and said they'd catch us up. He asked after Karen and I explained her arm was in plaster and she couldn't work – or worse, do her makeup.

"At least you can still hold your drink," Andy told her when she arrived.

Andy and I danced the evening away and he invited me to the Plaza cinema the following day. I said I'd love to go.

He walked me back to Woodside and kissed me on the cheek. "See you tomorrow," he said.

"I suppose you two are going steady now," said Shirley, as she arrived at Woodside just after Andy had left.

"I hope so," I said, feeling my heart flutter.

* * *

"We want to sit at the back, please," said Andy as the usherette showed us in. My heart had leapt when I'd seen him waiting for me outside. He was really happy as his aunt, who worked at the cinema, had given him complimentary tickets to see Whistle down the Wind starring Hayley Mills. The usherette shone her torch on two empty seats.

As the curtains went up, he put his arm around me. "Are you comfortable?" he asked.

"Yes, I'm fine. Are you?" I said, catching hold of his hand.

He gave my hand a squeeze. "I am now."

I was soon engrossed in the film and rested my head on his shoulder; I wanted to stay there forever. We arranged to meet again at the horse trough the following Wednesday before he kissed me goodnight.

"So where's your young man? Didn't he bring you home?" asked Miss Dickinson.

I felt myself blush. "We said goodnight at the bottom of the road," I said. "He's gone home now."

"No need for that, he could bring you to the door."

"Thanks, Miss Dickinson, I'll tell him." She smiled at me.

Two letters arrived for me a few days later. One was from Aunty Alice, the first I'd received from her since being put into care. The other was from Dad, who told me Mum was moving to a cottage hospital in St Austell, which meant I'd perhaps be able to visit her. I think social services had removed her from Fir Tree because they were concerned about the care she was getting. Although I was delighted I may get to see her, I felt sad that she had to leave her beloved cottage.

Aunty Alice asked if I wanted to spend Christmas with her and Uncle Will. I loved the idea and hoped it meant I could visit Mum with her. I longed to see Sam, too, but I didn't really hear much at all from him. He seemed content to let Dad write to me, and I feared Tim had convinced them both that I'd agreed with what he had done to me. I didn't ever get the chance to tell Sam the full extent of the abuse, as he became quite protective of Tim and I rarely saw him.

Work was going well, busy in the run-up to Christmas. But I

still had time to see Andy – nothing was going to stop me. He was happy about me having been invited to Aunty Alice's, as he knew how much I missed her and my family. I'd told Andy everything that had happened to me, from the beginning about my mum being ill and about how Tim had treated me.

"I'm pleased for you, but I'll miss you at Christmas," he said as we sat in a coffee bar called The Golden Dollar.

"I'll see you when I come back," I said, just as Only the Lonely by Roy Orbison came on the radio. We both laughed. "You'll be spending Christmas with your family, won't you?"

Andy nodded. "My mum, dad and sister," he said. "I'll take you to meet them after Christmas."

"I'd like that, how old is your sister?"

"Just turned fifteen, she's a right pain." I laughed. "I doubt it, I expect she's really nice," I said.

I saw Andy that Friday at youth club, then the following Wednesday. "I'm going to miss you," he said as we reached Woodside. Seeing I was torn, he added, "But you must go, your mum will want to see you. I'll be waiting for you when you come back."

He gave me a kiss. I'd found it so hard leaving him I was late in and feared that Miss Dickinson would tell me off. "Don't make a habit of it," was all she said.

Chapter Thirty-One

CATHY WAS GOING to her foster mother's for Christmas and we caught a train to St Austell together on Friday, December 22, 1961. I'd said goodbye to her at the station and was standing on the platform when I heard someone shout my name. "Christine! Christine!" I turned to see Aunty Alice running towards me. "Oh, it's so lovely having you home again," she said, hugging and kissing me.

She held me tight and it was wonderful to be with her after all this time. "I thought we'd see your mother before going home," she said.

"Can we really?"

She smiled at my excitement. "Of course," she said. "It's easier seeing her now she's in St Austell."

"I've got her a present, I hope she'll like it," I said. I had bought Mum a shawl from Spooners.

As we walked along the high street and up the hill to the hospital, Aunty Alice asked if I was all right. She asked about

Woodside and my job at Spooners. She asked why I hadn't told her about the abuse I'd suffered, but I still couldn't tell her how Tim had guns and had threatened to shoot her and Uncle Will, how he'd warned of a bloodbath. I'd promised my father.

"Christine, don't be upset if your mother doesn't seem to know you," she said as we entered the hospital. I was suddenly gripped by fear, wondering what state my poor mother was in by now.

We found her on a ward with several elderly ladies, a glass of water on a locker beside her bed. She looked as if she was fast asleep. I felt incredibly sad to see her lying there, looking so ill, her skin so pale, so lifeless. Emotion swept over me. Memories came flooding back. The heartbreak of leaving her in the way I did. How I'd had to deal with the worry of her being so ill, then having to deal with the ordeal of my brother's abuse. I felt a sudden panic, a fear of seeing Tim again and what he might do to me. No one knew how terrified of him I was, or the full extent of what I'd been through. Aunty Alice clearly didn't. I think Dad must have covered it up.

"Christine's here to see you, Ruby," she said. But Mum didn't stir.

"It's all right, I'll hold her hand," I said as Aunty Alice got some chairs.

I could feel tears well up as Mum wouldn't wake up. I was desperate to talk to her, to tell her about my job at Spooners, to tell her about Andy, my new friends and how I was wearing my hair. I wanted her to know I was okay and that even though I was far away, I was thinking of her all the time.

AN INNOCENT GIRL

"What shall I do with her present?" I asked Aunty Alice.

She looked in Mum's locker. "Put it in here. Your Dad will see it, then. We'll find her wearing it when we come in on Wednesday."

"I hope so," I said, squeezing my mother's hand. "I want you to know I've been here, Mum."

On the bus to Aunty Alice's I felt terribly sad to think I'd been sitting by my mother's side and she hadn't known I was there. Aunty Alice tried to reassure me that she'd be more awake on Wednesday when we planned to visit again.

Uncle Will was waiting for us when we got home and had the fire burning. It was a bitterly cold day and it was good to warm up. "I suppose you want one of Aunty Alice's pasties for tea?"

"Yes please, Uncle Will," I said. "I'd love one."

Aunty Alice laughed and headed for the kitchen. I felt really at home as I sat by the fire with the smell of pasties cooking.

Gazing out at the familiar view through the dining room window, wonderful memories of sitting with the family celebrating Victoria's engagement came flooding back to me.

"Is your pasty all right?" asked Uncle Will, his voice bringing me back to reality.

"It's lovely, thank you. I haven't tasted anything so good in ages."

Aunty Alice beamed at me. "Don't make them so good in Plymouth do they, my dear."

"No, yours are the best, Aunty Alice."

Lying in bed that night, I thought about all I'd been through, about the children's home and the kindness of Laura, about the girls and staff at Woodside. I felt so glad to be somewhere safe and not have to live with Tim and put up with any more of his abuse.

The next day the postman delivered a package for me. "Andy's sent me a beautiful necklace, Aunty Alice!" I squealed in delight. "And a lovely Christmas card, look!"

I still have the Christmas card to this day, although it's not far off 60 years old now and more than a little discoloured.

She was thrilled for me. "We're going to have to meet this Andy of yours," she said.

We had a wonderful Christmas, with neighbours and family calling round. I was so happy when Dad arrived on his bike on Boxing Day to wish me a Merry Christmas and give me a hug. "I wrapped the shawl you gave your mother around her shoulders," he said as we sat around the table for tea.

"I thought I'd take Christine in to see her again tomorrow," Aunty Alice told Dad.

"Yes, best Christine sees her as much as she can," he replied.

When we went in the following day, I found Mum propped up in bed and gave her a cuddle. "Do you like your shawl, Mum? Is it keeping you warm?"

She gave me a little smile, a smile that meant the world. I was over the moon, so relieved that she was awake and knew I was there.

"It's lovely and warm," said Aunty Alice.

I kissed Mum and sat beside her. Aunty Alice and I chatted about all the Christmas decorations on the ward and pointed at the tree that lit up in the far corner. Mum looked towards it.

"I think she enjoyed the carols yesterday evening," the lady in the next bed told us.

"Did you enjoy the carols, Ruby?" asked Aunty Alice. Mum managed a little nod.

I was so happy and gave her another kiss. I didn't say anything about what had happened to me, where I'd been all this time. I had no idea what Dad might have told her. The truth was concealed from her to save her the upset of knowing. She was too ill to deal with it.

I caught the train back to Plymouth with Cathy on the 28th. We were sad to leave the people we loved, and comforted each other as best we could. I was sad, too, that I hadn't seen Sam. I was grateful to him for helping me get away, but he was supporting Tim now and in truth, I hadn't expected him to visit me. Cathy showed me two nighties her foster mother had given her, and I showed her my necklace from Andy, kept safely in its box as I wanted to wait until our date on the Friday before wearing it.

It was great to see the girls back at the home. Shirley and Ben had got engaged and she showed us her lovely ring. "When will you get married?" I asked.

"I'll need my dad's permission, but we're hoping in the summer," she said. "Ben will apply for married quarters, so we'll have somewhere to live."

"You're so lucky, it sounds like a dream come true," I said, suddenly feeling envious.

"Your turn will come," she said smiling. "I can imagine you

marrying Andy."

"I can't wait to see him," I said.

* * *

Youth club was cancelled that Friday because of the snow, but Miss Dickinson said I could bring Andy back to the home. I couldn't wait, but boredom had set in that afternoon as we all sat around unsure what do with ourselves. Laura suggested making a snowman. "Yes, we'll go across the road and build it on the lawn," said Cathy excitedly.

We were soon in our coats and gloves rushing towards the garden. Susan watched us out of the window. I gave her a wave. "Ask Miss Cavell if she's got a carrot we can use for a nose," Laura called out to her.

I went to the door to collect it. "Thanks," I said when Susan brought one out. She looked pleased.

"Nice to be able to help, even if it's only a little," she said handing me the carrot. "You know I'm due to have my baby next week, don't you?"

"Yes, Laura told me. At least you'll get it over," I said trying to comfort her.

"I suppose so," she said quietly, sadness etched on her face. "I can't wait to go home."

I stepped inside and hugged her. "I'll be over to see you soon," I said as I left. She was soon back looking out of the window, watching us having fun.

"I like your snowman, girls," called Mrs Mann from a bedroom window. We smiled up at her. "You can come in and help make the beds after," she joked.

"No thanks," we called back, before searching for black stones for his eyes.

"I say, he looks pretty good," said Laura once the snowman was complete. "What shall we call him?"

"What about Jack?" I asked, thinking of Jack Frost. I felt a snowball hit me and spun around.

"I should have known it was you, Karen," I said, before throwing one back. She dodged and it hit a bush.

"You need to be a lot better shot to get me," she taunted as she ran off.

"She thinks she got away with it, but I'll get her later on," I said, as Laura and Cathy grinned.

We went back in cold but happy.

I met Andy at the horse trough as usual. We hugged and kissed before walking back up to Woodside with his arm around me.

We were barely through the door when Miss Dickinson asked if he was any good with electrics and if he could repair her bedside light. I was so proud he could help her. He asked if he could take me to the cinema the following evening and Miss Dickinson agreed.

I walked Andy to the front door and told him that Aunty Alice wanted him to meet her and my mum. "Yes, I'd like that. We'll talk about it tomorrow," he said.

I felt a warm glow. "Did you notice our snowman?" I asked after we kissed. "Doesn't he look nice with the street light on him, glistening in the dark?"

Andy turned to look before smiling and kissing me again. "You made a good job of it," he said.

"Hurry up and shut the door, Christine. You're letting the cold in," Miss Dickinson called out.

"I'll be up for you at seven," said Andy as he walked away.

When we met the next day to go to the cinema, Andy said he was free to visit Aunty Alice and my mother the following Saturday.

"I'd love that!" I squealed. "I'll write to let Aunty Alice know."

I'd been knitting myself a mohair cardigan and Andy complimented me on it when I took my coat off. "It feels ever so soft," he said, cuddling into me.

The curtains went up and we were soon engrossed in the film, and despite the wintry conditions outside we still had ice cream during the interval.

On the Wednesday evening, I told Andy that Aunty Alice had confirmed Saturday. "What about meeting my family now?" he said.

"What, you mean this evening?"

He nodded. "Yes, I've gone on about you so much they can't wait to see you."

"I hope they like me," I said.

It wasn't far to Andy's house, and I felt nervous as he opened the door. "I've brought Christine to see you," he called out.

"Come in, come in, we've been looking forward to meeting you," a man that I presumed to be his father shouted back.

The house was warm and welcoming, a lovely log fire

burning in the grate. I was invited to sit on the settee beside the fire and Andy sat next me. His mother made me a cup of tea and Andy introduced me to his dog Queenie, a Kerry blue terrier with a blue-black curly coat.

As I smoothed Queenie Andys' sister Phyllis smiled. "Did you like your necklace?" she asked. "The one Andy sent you at Christmas?"

"Yes, it was lovely. I've got it on now." I took off my coat to show her.

"That's good. He sent me down town to buy it," she said.

"Did he?" I was surprised. "It's beautiful, I love it."

"What did you have to tell her that for, Phyllis?" said Andy. "I wanted Christine to think I chose it."

"It's all right, I understand," I said. I wasn't disappointed, just pleased he'd been kind enough to buy me a necklace. His sister grinned.

"Coronation Street is on in a minute," said his mother. "Do you watch it?"

"Yes, when I've got the chance," I told her. She looked pleased.

"Where do you work?" asked Phyllis.

"Spooners in the office."

She looked interested.

"You've just started work haven't you, sis?" Andy prompted.

"She's got a nice job at Berketex making dresses," their father said proudly.

"I've only been there a couple of weeks," said Phyllis, "I'm just training."

I smiled at her. "That sounds nice."

Coronation Street came on and Andy began making a fuss of Queenie. "I was only a little boy when we got her," he told me. "I carried her all the way home from the Barbican."

I could tell how much he loved her.

"She's getting old now," said his father, who was called Andrew.

"I've never had a dog, only chickens, turkeys, geese and ducks," I said.

His father nodded. "Yes, Andy was telling us that you're from Cornwall."

"Well, we'd better get you home," said Andy looking at the clock. I smoothed Queenie one more time before getting up.

"Come for tea one Sunday if you like," said his mother, Hilda, as I was about to leave.

"Do you want to?" asked Andy.

"Yes please, I'd like that."

"So, what do you think of them? Do you like them?" asked Andy once we were outside.

"Yes, they're really nice, so friendly," I said. It had been a lovely visit.

When I got back to the home, I was devastated to learn that Susan had left. Her baby had been taken and she was dreadfully upset. I couldn't even write to her as she'd left no forwarding address for me. I was welcoming new people into my life, but I didn't want to forget the people I'd already met, those who had supported me and been my true friends.

Chapter Thirty-Two

MUM WAS LOOKING very poorly when Andy and I arrived at the hospital. She didn't seem to recognise me.

"Christine's brought her boyfriend to see you, Ruby," said Aunty Alice. "He's called Andy."

Andy stepped forward and, to my surprise, Mum gave him a lovely smile.

"It looks as if she likes you, Andy," said Aunty Alice. I sat beside Mum and held her hand as Aunty Alice began talking to Andy. "She's been poorly for a long time," she said.

He nodded. "I think it was really nice she gave me such a lovely smile," he said.

We stayed with Mum for several hours. When it was time to go, I told Mum we'd be down to see her again soon and kissed her on the cheek. She didn't respond.

"It's a pity your mum's so poorly," said Andy sadly as we headed back for the railway station. "I feel sure she was asking me to take care of you when she gave me that smile."

His words almost made me cry. I was so glad he wanted to take care of me, and so pleased Mum had smiled so sweetly at him.

We talked a lot on the train, and I opened up even more about how things had been. He put his arm around me and held me tight.

At first, Andy found it hard to take in and thought of Tim as a deeply sick man, but as time passed, his focus was mainly on me as a person and on our future together and less on my past. "At least you're safe now you've got away from Tim," he would say. I was so relieved he understood.

Dad came to Plymouth a few weeks later and I was delighted to see him and Andy getting on well. Things were really falling into place. I felt happy, content. I felt safe.

Until Miss Wilkins called me into her office.

"I'm terribly sorry, Christine," she said, "but your father phoned earlier to say your mother has passed away."

My heart sunk. I gasped with dismay.

"Sit down, my dear," said Miss Wilkins, helping me over to the settee. "Do you want a cup of tea?"

I felt weak and sank into the seat. Miss Wilkins sat next to me her arm around my shoulder.

"Yes please," I spluttered as my mouth went dry.

She rang the bell to summon someone from the kitchen. "Could you please bring Christine a cup of tea?" she asked when Miss Cavell appeared. Miss Cavell nodded and looked so sorry for me.

I burst into tears.

"Are you feeling well enough to go back over to Southview?" asked Miss Wilkins after I'd sipped my tea and regained some semblance of composure.

"I think so."

"Miss Dickinson has been told, she'll take care of you," said Miss Wilkins.

I felt as if the bottom of my world had dropped out, my mind in complete turmoil.

"I'm going to my room," I said to Miss Dickinson when she asked how I was.

She nodded. "I'm here for you, don't forget that." She put her arm on my shoulder. "Come and see me if you want to talk."

I choked up. "I... I think I want to be on my own at the moment," I whispered.

Miss Dickinson brought me a cup of tea and an aspirin after a while. "It might help," she said when I took it.

I lay in bed sobbing and must have cried myself to sleep as I woke to find Cathy sitting next to me. When she saw my sad face, she gave me a hug.

Andy tried to comfort me when we met that evening. I was so upset, my mind all over the place. Thoughts of the funeral raced through my head. I knew Aunty Alice and Uncle Will would be there, which reassured me. I felt sick about losing my mother. I felt it was all so unfair, on her, on me... on all of us. I wished she'd never had a stroke and that all this hadn't happened.

"Aunty Alice wants you to stay with her so you can go to the funeral together," Miss Wilkins told me the next day. "You could wear your black skirt and cardigan, but you could do with getting a hat."

A hat was the furthest thing from my mind. Mrs Brown took me shopping, but I couldn't find any black hats I liked. I spotted a powder blue one made of feathers which I did like, but Mrs Brown didn't approve and tried to persuade me not to buy it.

"It wouldn't just be for the funeral. I could wear it to church," I said to persuade her.

"All right, if you think so," she said, not wanting to argue with me.

Back at Woodside Miss Wilkins didn't say anything, but she didn't look impressed. "I couldn't persuade Christine to get a black one," said Mrs Brown.

* * *

"Ashes to ashes, dust to dust..." Tears streamed down my face as the vicar spoke. It was May 2, 1963, a day I'll never forget. I found the funeral traumatic and stood motionless between Aunty Alice and Uncle Will as I watched my mother's body being lowered into the ground. I was aware of Tim looking at me from the other side of the grave. Dad and Sam stood with him, looking sad.

"Anyone would think you were at wedding, Christine, wearing a hat like that," chided Aunty Maisie as she threw earth down on the coffin. I didn't know her very well; she was the wife of Dad's cousin. But her words shocked and upset me. Aunty Alice put her arm around me and led me away.

"Don't take any notice, dear. That was a stupid thing to say," she whispered.

"We're going back to yours aren't we, Alice?" asked Mum's cousin. Aunty Alice nodded.

"We won't come back, Alice, we'll go on home," said Dad as we left.

I needed Dad to comfort me and felt abandoned by him. It seemed as if he, Tim and Sam had each other while I was on my own. Back at Aunty Alice's, I went to a bedroom and wept into a pillow for the whole afternoon. I felt so lonely, unable to have close contact with Dad or Sam because of the situation. I felt they both closed ranks to protect Tim and I was left to fend for myself. They'd looked extremely sad at the funeral, like me, but I wasn't able to share my grief with them.

"We'll always be here for you," said Aunty Alice, kissing me goodbye before I got a train back to Plymouth the following morning.

Chapter Thirty-Three

A LETTER CAME from Dad. He had good news, he wrote. He was getting married. Included was an invitation for Andy and me to attend the wedding. It was just over a year since Mum died. I felt so sad, but at the same time happy for him. I knew how lonely he'd been, how much he'd struggled to look after her for so long.

Andy and I attended the wedding, but I couldn't help feeling a distance between myself and Dad's new family. I know now that Dad never told my stepmother Elsie the truth about me being taken away from home, in need of care and protection. It seems she knew something had happened between Tim and myself, but had been given the idea that I was to blame for leading him on.

I know this must have been the case because I overheard her saying, "She offered it to him on a plate, what man would refuse that?" and I knew she was talking about me.

It was what she'd been told about me. She perhaps wasn't aware that I was only twelve when the abuse started, and Tim was twenty-four.

After this I didn't visit them very much. If I did visit, my step-mother's attitude was cold and hostile and she made me feel unwelcomed. My father was always glad to see me, but she was in charge and he did what he was told.

I was always treated nicely by my stepsister Jenny she was kind whenever she saw me. I really appreciated that. It made me feel happier about visiting Dad and I'll always be grateful to her. My father didn't want his new family to know the truth, so, along with Sam, he covered it up. He didn't want them to think badly of him for not being able to look after and protect his young daughter.

I feel sorry for Dad. I know he was weak, but this was due to his own difficult childhood. His father, a Methodist lay preacher, used to give him and his brothers the double rope across their bottoms if they misbehaved or did anything wrong. He often said villagers would tell tales on them to get them into trouble. The scars of those beatings left their mark and broke his spirit.

Not long after the wedding, Miss Wilkins called me into the office.

"Your social worker is saying it's time you looked for lodgings," she said.

She looked really sad – and I must have looked shocked. I was still just seventeen years old and hadn't thought about leaving Woodside.

"Do you know anywhere?" she asked.

I shook my head. "No, not really, I'll ask the girls at work."

The prospect of leaving was daunting but also, once it had

sunk in, exciting. At lunchtime in the canteen, I began asking around. One girl said her aunt and uncle had a boarding house at West Hoe and said she'd call them to see if they had room for me. Mr and Mrs Gates did, indeed, have a room, so I went to meet them with my social worker Miss Lucas, who explained how social services would help me with the rent.

Mrs Gates was lovely. From the day I moved in she invited me to have meals with her and her husband. I was treated like one of the family – they had no children of their own. Cathy from the home moved in soon afterwards, and we travelled to work together. I'd left Spooners by now and was working at Farley's with Cathy.

With my 18th birthday just days away, I received a letter from social services informing me they'd no longer be able to help with my rent. I'd taken a job at Farley's because they paid better wages, but I still had real concerns about affording it on my own.

Dad had arranged to visit me with Elsie on my birthday, so I met them at the bus station in the city centre. He asked what I'd like as a birthday present and I showed him an imitation leopard skin coat that was the latest fashion. My stepmother didn't look pleased when he bought it and told me "That's the last thing you'll get from your father. He's married to me now and I want my sons to have new things."

I didn't say anything. I looked over at Dad, who just stood there looking sheepish, clearly feeling unable to do anything about it.

"Never mind, you've got me now," said Andy when I told

him about it. But I felt I'd lost my dad and had been finally and completely pushed out.

A card from Miss Lucas arrived the day after my birthday telling me I was officially out of care and sending me her best wishes.

"I can't save anything now. I have to pay so much rent," I told Andy. "By the time I pay for my lodgings and bus fares to work I'm left with nothing."

He nodded. "Yes, and most of my money goes to Mum." His father had been taken ill and was unable to work, and Andy was expected to help out more.

"It'll take us ages to save up to get married," I said, consumed by sadness.

Andy hugged me. "Why don't I ask my parents if you can move in with us?"

"Would you do that?" My spirits were lifted with a simple nod of his head.

Andy's mother agreed to take me in for much less than I was paying at the boarding house. I was sorry to leave Cathy, but we still saw each other every day at work.

Andy must have managed to save some money at least, because he soon took me down town so I could choose an engagement ring. I knew he couldn't afford much, so didn't look for anything too expensive. I chose a gold ring with a solitaire diamond in a platinum setting. I felt so proud to be wearing it.

When I told Dad we wanted to get married he agreed to give me £50 in premium bonds, which he said had belonged to Mum. "Think of it as a wedding present from your Mum," he said, handing it over. I knew it was the only way he was able give me anything and felt quite sad about it.

We were to be married at the registry office as we couldn't afford a church wedding. I bought a powder-blue skirt and jacket and a white handbag and sandals.

"Everything will be all right," said Andy, switching the radio on. Ruby Murray was singing, "We don't need a fancy wedding, on a special day in spring. All we need is real love, wrapped up in a tiny ring."

"Sounds as if that song's meant for us," he said.

We found a flat on Mutley Plain and got ready to move in. I was really excited as our wedding day got nearer.

On July 2, 1965 the big day arrived. I had my hair done at the hairdressers. I put on my trusted Max Factor Tempting Touch face powder, pale pink lipstick and a dash of Panache perfume.

I arrived at the registry office with Dad, my stepmother and Aunty Alice who came on her own because Uncle Will was working. Andy was already there waiting for me, having been driven in his best man Michael's Austin Mini. Cathy and some friends from work were there too, but there was no Sam. Our wedding was a quiet affair but seemed really wonderful to me. The sun shone brightly on the happiest day of my life.

"We're Mr and Mrs at last!" said Andy as he kissed me after the ceremony. I felt so happy to have tied the knot. I felt Tim wouldn't be able to hurt me now I was a married woman. Everyone came back for a buffet I'd prepared at the flat as we couldn't afford anything else – but we all enjoyed it.

We didn't live at the flat for long as Andy's parents moved to a bigger house and asked if we'd like to move in with them. We did; they lived downstairs and we lived on the first floor.

"I'll take care of you," Andy promised me. For the first time in ages I felt safe and secure.

Chapter Thirty-Four

THERE WAS A knock on the door and Andy's mother went to answer. A man explained how he was my brother and she let him in. It was Tim. Just the sound of his voice was enough to fill me with dread.

"I've just been down to see father," he told us. "But my gearbox is giving me trouble and I don't think I'll be able to make it back to London."

Andy's mother wasn't aware of the abuse I'd suffered at the hands of my brother. A year had passed since our wedding, and he was living in Sutton with Sam. I just wanted him to leave. Andy knew I didn't want Tim anywhere near me, and he thought it best to fix the van so he wouldn't have any excuse for staying.

"I've managed to get another gearbox. Do you think you could fit it for me?" Tim asked Andy.

Andy took me aside away from Tim. "What should I do, Christine?"

"Just get his car fixed," I said. "You're right. It'll be the quickest way to get rid of him."

Andy's friend Rick was there and offered to help. "Take care mind, and don't trust him," I told Andy. I had seen Tim try to kill my mother, threaten to throw me from a moving car and run over a policeman's foot. I knew he didn't care what he did or who he hurt.

"I will, don't worry about me," said Andy. "I'll put some bricks under the van when it's jacked up to make sure it can't fall on us."

I hated Tim hanging around me as they worked on the van. I felt so uncomfortable having him in the house, but at least I felt safer with Andy's parents there. He tried to make conversation, but I can't remember what we talked about. I found the experience utterly traumatic.

"I'll go and see how they're getting on," he said after a while. I nodded, desperate for him to go.

I soon heard Andy shout, "Get out of it, you stupid bastard!"

I rushed outside. "He's only let the handbrake off with us underneath," shouted Andy. He was furious. He and Rick had shot out from under the van, both looking bewildered at what Tim had done.

"Good job you put those bricks under it," said Rick looking shaken. "I felt the van rock and knew something was happening."

Tim looked furtive and skulked away. "That idiot tried to kill us," screamed Andy, before turning to Rick. "Let's get this gearbox in so he can shove off again."

I stared at Tim. Andy was the person I loved and trusted the most in the world, and now my brother had tried to kill him. I now realise in Tim's crazy, mixed-up mind he believed if he could get rid of Andy, I'd have to live with him.

In that moment, I understood that I had done the right thing leaving home. Tim would have never left and, even if he were forced to leave, he would have never stayed away.

I didn't care anymore that Dad never heard my side of the story, even if he were persuaded that I had been in agreement to be abused.

Years later, I found out that Tim was mad at Sam, wanting to kill him for not bringing me back home once I was taken over by social services. Tim was in such a state that Sam had to dismantle the engine of his van to stop him coming to look for me.

"Why did you let off the handbrake with them underneath?" I screamed at Tim. I could see he looked upset because his plan hadn't worked.

Andy was working quickly on the van. "Here, it's done; it should get you back to London," he said.

Tim got into the driver's seat. "I didn't mean to do it," he said before he left. Andy looked at him with utter contempt.

Andy said later. "He could have had us both trapped underneath."

I gave him a hug. "I'd never forgive him if he hurt you."

"I think it's made me realise what you've been up against," he said, holding me close.

"I never want him here again," I said.

Andy nodded. "Don't worry. He won't come near you again with me around."

I felt so glad to hear him say that.

Chapter Thirty-Five

ANDY AND I went on to have two daughters, Angela and Susie, and later became foster carers, looking after 140 teenagers over 23 years. We had planned to foster only girls, having had two of our own, but boys were harder to place so we were persuaded to take them instead. Some had been remanded into the care of the local authority by the courts after having turned to crime.

"I'd like to help them stay out of trouble," I told Andy, explaining what had happened to Sam. He agreed and wanted to help these young lads onto the right path.

Dad died on Christmas Day 1980, aged 72.

He suffered a cardiac arrest and was taken to Bodmin hospital. Jenny, my step-sister, phoned to let me know. Both my brothers visited him, arriving at his bedside before me. My Dad looked enormously relieved to see me when I arrived. Thankfully, my brothers had left by this time.

"I was afraid you wouldn't come to see me, love," he said as I sat on the chair beside his bed.

"Why?" I asked. "You should know I'd always be here."

"I thought you wouldn't come to see me because of Tim being here," he told me.

"Of course I would, nothing would stop me seeing you," I reassured him as I caught hold his hand.

"I want to ask you something, love," he said looking really concerned.

"What is it?" I asked as I could see something was troubling him.

"Could you please be nice to Tim once I'm gone? He's not got anyone else love, only you and Sam."

I stayed silent and sobbed, looking at this helpless man. I could see it meant a lot to him a request for reconciliation.

"If anything happens to Sam," he looked imploringly at me, "Tim won't have anyone." He was choked up.

"I'll keep in touch with them Dad," I promised as I bent over to give him a kiss.

On Christmas Day I received the dreaded phone call telling me my father had passed away.

I saw my brothers at his funeral and gave Sam my phone number so he could keep in contact. He usually called on Sunday evenings, and they both seemed happy and enjoying their lives together. He often passed me over to speak to Tim, who had now become more accepting of me being married to Andy.

When Sam was made redundant in 1985, he bought a house in Yorkshire for himself and Tim. I felt glad knowing they had somewhere to live and that they were together. Sam had a girlfriend, Eileen, but never married her because he felt too much responsibility for Tim.

It was 1996 when Tim phoned to say Sam had gone into hospital for a heart bypass operation. Fortunately, he recovered, and they carried on enjoying life together, attending car boot sales and visiting antique dealers in their local area. "We're making brooches and selling them," Sam was proud to tell me during one of his Sunday evening calls.

I was terribly sad when Tim phoned to tell me Sam had passed away on October 23, 2000. I wasn't able to attend his funeral because of fostering commitments.

The next call came in 2004. "Your brother Tim's had a stroke," said a care worker. "We can't let him go home because his house is in such a state."

I was concerned and asked Andy what we should do. Ever practical, and ever kind, he suggested we go and see what the situation was. "If it needs cleaning we can do it, can't we?" I asked. He nodded.

Seeing Tim was a shock. He was 71 and seemed to have physically shrunk. Looking weak and completely helpless, I realised he was no longer a threat.

"Can you help me, Christine?" he asked. "They're saying I'll have to go in a care home."

He was a pitiful sight. Tears filled my eyes and compassion overwhelmed me. I could only think of the time he looked after Mum when she had her stroke.

"We'll do our best," Andy told him. Tim looked so relieved.

His house was, indeed, a mess, with rubbish piled high and newspapers, boxes and bags strewn everywhere. We got bin bags and began to fill them. We couldn't work out where Tim had been sleeping as even the bed was covered in junk.

"He was found lying under the sink," a neighbour told us. "I didn't think he'd survive. It'll take you weeks to clean up that mess."

I felt a bit like 'Joseph' in the story of 'Joseph and his coat of many Colours' which my father used to tell me. After being treated badly by his brothers Joseph helped them out when there was a famine. I feel this is what has happened with me being kind and helpful to my brother at the end of the day.

Andy and I worked morning and night.

Under Tim's bed, there something that looked like a home-made crossbow.

"They made this to use with this contraption," Andy said, showing me some sort of weird mechanism which they used as a man trap to catch a burglar if one dared to break in. Pair of odd balls they were," he concluded after a moment of silence in which we stared at the crossbow and the man trap.

"What's in this?" I wondered when I saw a bottle beside Tim's bed.

"It says cyanide," said Andy. "What's he doing with that?"

"I expect he uses it for testing gold" I said, remembering him doing it at Fir Tree when I was a child.

"Don't knock it over, put it somewhere safe," said Andy. "We need to replace the sink. It looks as if he's been peeing in it."

I looked at it and shuddered, then called a plumber.

"I think we'd better contact the police to get the cyanide removed," said Andy.

Police and council officers were soon there. "We'll have to board up the house for now," a council official told us. "You'll have to pay for the cyanide to be removed by a specialist team."

"How much will that cost?" I asked, suddenly worried about money again.

It turned out to be £250, with a team in white boiler suits and protective gear needed for the job.

"Fancy Tim's been sleeping with that cyanide bottle right under his nose," I said to Andy.

"What a state to be living in," he said.

With the cyanide safely removed, Andy and I bought Tim a television and arranged for carers to come in.

"He's been diagnosed with Diogenes Syndrome," the staff nurse at the hospital told me. "It's a condition often discovered when people are found living in squalor."

We stocked up Tim's cupboards and ensured he had enough food. "You've done a good job," said one of his carers.

Tim was really grateful to be able to return home. "Do you think you can send me up a Cornish pasty?" he asked before we left.

"And some saffron buns I suppose," said Andy with a grin.

Tim passed away in 2009 aged 75. I felt a mixture of sadness and relief, because since Sam passed away, I'd felt responsible for him. It was daunting coming to terms with the fact I was the only remaining member of my birth family.

I felt sorry for my poor dad who had nursed both Mum and my stepmother after they suffered strokes. He had his faults, but I knew Dad was a good kind man who was just unable to look after me. I also knew if Mum had been well none of this would have happened. Without her to oversee things, Dad was pretty useless. My brothers were stronger characters than him and he was unable to deal with the situation when I told him about Tim. Dad was far too scared to challenge him about it. The presence of the guns played a big part; my mother would never have allowed it.

I felt able to help Tim in later years because he was frail, weak and helpless. I can't say I ever forgave him for what he did to me. I just did what I considered right, treating him with kindness in his final hour of need. He was powerless in the end.

I concluded many years ago that he wasn't a well person and had mental health problems, undiagnosed and untreated. I have never been able to completely forget the abuse and there have been times when I have experienced flashbacks. I'm very aware it's had an effect on me and caused significant problems in my life. As time goes by the flashbacks have become less frequent, less traumatic, which has been very much to do with Andy's kindness and understanding. My two lovely daughters have also been a huge help. They've both been extremely caring and supportive. I have been lucky in many ways to have such a loving and understanding family.

I still love Sam, too, and feel eternally grateful he helped me get away. I have no idea what I would have done if he hadn't. I was thinking about running away or taking my own life, which would have meant my story never being told.

THE END

Epilogue

"IF ONLY HE hadn't abused me," I said as we drove home from Tim's funeral.

We'd arranged everything, a task that had brought back many memories I'd rather forget. I felt huge sadness that I hadn't been able to have a normal brother and sister relationship with him.

Andy nodded. "Yes, but if you hadn't come to Plymouth, you wouldn't have met me."

"I know," I said. "But I still wish it had never happened."

"Sam and Tim are together again now," said Andy, trying to comfort me. "You carried out Tim's wishes by sprinkling his ashes with Sam's in the garden of rest."

"Yes, I suppose so," I said, tears trickling down my face.

We stopped at a service station and sat at a table. "You're the best husband I could ever have had," I said.

"You think so?" said Andy, looking amused.

I nodded. "I know so. Who else would put up with me?"

He started laughing. "You were in the tea leaves. It was meant to be," he said.

And I couldn't help laughing too.

Special Thanks

I WOULD LIKE to give praise to Cornwall Social Services for taking me into care and making sure I was looked after. I am so grateful for this because it was a relief to know I wouldn't have to put up with the abuse any longer. I would like to thank Miss Lucas and Miss Watkins, who dealt with my case, for being so kind and understanding. I am also very grateful to Miss Wilkins and Miss Dickinson, who really cared about the girls they were looking after at Woodside and Southview. I regret now that I didn't thank them enough at the time or show my appreciation. The same goes for Mrs Brown and Mrs Mann, care workers at the home who were so helpful and supportive. And the girls I met at the home and had so much fun with – Sandy and Karen for doing my hair and giving me advice on makeup; Shirley, who was a great inspiration to me talking about her lovely boyfriend, Ben. To all the girls living at Woodside and Southview at the time, I really enjoyed your company and laughter. Later on in life, I managed to get back in touch with some of my wonderful school friends, and I thank them too. A big thank you to Marnie Summerfield Smith. Her kindness and empathy has helped me find my voice. After years of remaining silent I've felt able to speak. Marnie's been a star shining in the dark. Thank you also to Dyfed Edwards for his part in helping me publish my book.

Printed in Great Britain
by Amazon